Learning to Teach Drama

Learning to Teach Drama

A CASE NARRATIVE APPROACH

Edited by
Joe Norris, Laura A. McCammon, and Carole S. Miller

HEINEMANN
Portsmouth, NH

Heinemann
A division of Reed Elsevier Inc.
361 Hanover Street
Portsmouth, NH 03801–3912
www.heinemann.com

Offices and agents throughout the world

Library of Congress Cataloging-in-Publication Data
Learning to teach drama : a case narrative approach / edited by Joe Norris, Laura A. McCammon, and Carole S. Miller.
    p. cm.
    Includes bibliographical references.
    ISBN 0-325-00228-2 (alk. paper)
    1. Drama—Study and teaching (Secondary). I. Norris, Joe.
II. McCammon, Laura A. III. Miller, Carole S.
    PN1701.L43 2000
    809.2'0071'2—dc21

                      99-087989

Editor: Lisa A. Barnett
Production: Elizabeth Valway
Cover design: Joni Doherty Design
Manufacturing: Louise Richardson

Printed in the United States of America on acid-free paper
04 03 02 01 00   DA 1 2 3 4 5

Contents

Foreword

It seems particularly appropriate to comment on a new teacher case-book devoted to the teaching and learning of drama. There is a natural affinity between drama and cases. Cases are narratives. They have a beginning, a middle, and an end. Cases are inherently dramatic. They invite attention, identification, and the investment of interest and emotion precisely because they have well-developed plots, interesting characters, and elements of tension and uncertainty. Indeed, the very word *case* derives etymologically from the idea of "chance." We say to a friend that we should plan to meet at the big clock at 2:00 P.M., "just in case" we become separated while shopping. In teacher education we are often accused of being overly abstract and theoretical on the one hand and also of being far too concrete and "mickey mouse" on the other hand. But case-based teaching, as it has been used in business, education, public policy, medicine, and other fields, may permit us to be both concretely situated and theoretically disposed at the same time.

During the past decade, teacher educators and scholars all over the world have paid increased attention to case-based teaching as a way to enrich teacher education and professional development. Instead of separating theory and practice, as typically occurs in teacher education, learning with cases bridges the gap between these domains. It involves actively reflecting on and examining problematic situations in the real world of practice, often testing theoretical propositions and/or generating new ones. Analyzing and discussing cases can prepare prospective and veteran teachers to become problem solvers who pose questions, frame and reframe problems, explore multiple perspectives, and examine alternative solutions. In short, case-based teaching can help neophytes learn to think like a teacher and can promote communities of learners among veterans.

The typical case depicts a problem, dilemma, or crisis that has occurred in a teacher's class. Something that the teacher planned has gone awry—whether a "problem of the day," an attempt to try a new lesson, or an effort to expand students' appreciation of diverse cultures. Students have become confused, have utterly missed the point, or have grown upset at the teacher's offers of assistance. And the teacher has reached a point where she or he just doesn't know what to do. The case vividly describes the events that led up to the problem, the classroom context in which the situation occurred, and the ways in which the teacher attempted to set matters on course. Some cases, like those in this excellent volume, are followed by a series of commentaries that can enrich analyses of the narrative.

The editors of this volume do not write the cases themselves. Building from a tradition that began with our *Intern Teacher Casebook* (Shulman and Colbert 1988), the editors engage directly and personally with a number of teachers in reconstructing episodes from their own experience and authoring their own case narratives, written in the first person. In contrast to the professional case writers who prepare business school cases, for example, or the law professors who write legal cases, these writers are the protagonists who experienced the events and emotions associated with each case. The teachers not only write their own cases, they assist one another, comment on each other's cases, and effectively create a learning community in the process. Thus, not only is the product educative, the process provides a professionally enriching experience for the authors and editors themselves.

I met two of the editors a few years ago when I attended a session on their case project at an American Educational Research Association (AERA) meeting in New York. At that time, I was impressed both with their use of Readers' Theatre as the medium of their presentation and with the content of their cases, and I encouraged them to pursue publication. There were no—and are no—cases embedded in drama education, and I thought they would contribute to the growing case literature in education. Little did I know that three years later they would ask me write this foreword for their casebook; nor had I realized the extent to which my husband Lee Shulman and I had contributed to their endeavor.

From an e-mail message that Laura wrote earlier this year, I learned that Joe had first heard about the importance of cases in the early 1990s from Lee in a presentation to a group of Canadian teacher educators and had used my co-edited cases on diversity in his drama education courses (Shulman and Mesa-Bains 1993). He also had his students write their own cases about their experiences teaching drama and got permission from them to use their cases with other groups of students, and this project was born. In subsequent years, Joe's students continued to write new cases and respond to old ones. Thus he was able to develop quite an extensive case library for his students on issues directly related to drama education.

At about the same time, I conducted a series of seminars on case-based teaching at Arizona State University, engaging folks in provocative case discussions and examining the benefits of case-based teaching to both the discussion participants and case authors. Laura reminded me that she had been assigned as my graduate assistant host and became intrigued with using cases in her own teaching. So she was primed to use them in her own teaching and work with Joe and Carole as each of them experimented with cases at his or her respective institution. During the past four years, these educators have collaborated with one another: working with students to write new cases, field-testing the cases in one another's classrooms, soliciting commentaries from other students and from their cooperating teachers, and studying their practice. This book and the articles and presentations the editors have generated are a result of that collaboration.

In her message to me, Laura referred to Lee and me as "sort of the parents of this project." After reading their outstanding manuscript, I feel honored to have that distinction. Parents take pride in seeing their children take an idea and make it their own. These educators have definitely transformed our ideas and improved upon them. Their students' cases are detailed, compelling, and sometimes poignant accounts that depict neophytes examining dilemmas they encountered as they tried to teach drama to their students. But these narratives are not just stories of neophytes' struggles. They are educative because they are cases of something, exemplars of a class or instances of a larger category. Their themes represent difficulties that all novices have experienced, such as planning inappropriate instruction, teaching apparently unmotivated students, providing inadequate scaffolding for assignments, and developing trust with difficult students.

What makes this set of narratives unique, however, is its setting in drama education. The cases and accompanying commentaries by other new and veteran teachers enable readers to appreciate the particularities and major issues of this special field. Teachers preparing to be drama teachers can vicariously learn how to think like a drama teacher by examining the authors' dilemmas and the conversations among the commentators. The "Extensions" section that follows each case consists of questions and activities designed by the editors to help with this analysis. They encourage the readers to go beyond each narrative and relate the situations to their own teaching.

As we read through these cases, we are reminded of several ways in which cases about the teaching and learning of drama can be of value to all educators. We can think of at least five reasons: public performance, collaboration, literacy, morality, and emotion. First, drama is closely identified with public performance. In an era when many educators are recognizing the power of performance and "publicness" in all fields, drama can be a valuable resource for us all. We hear repeated calls for performance assessment, displaying achievement through public exhibitions, and communities of learners who perform their understandings in consequential ways, such as making reports to the local town council. Second, drama is in principle collaborative and interdependent, both on stage and in back of it. At a time when educators, political leaders, and business executives all value collaborative learning and the development of learning communities, we will find few models as valuable as those in drama. Third, drama occupies naturally the intersection of written and spoken literacy, two of the most important domains of learning for all students. Fourth, most fine dramas engage actors and audience in wrestling with fundamental moral and ethical dilemmas. These are critical domains that present educators with difficult pedagogical dilemmas when addressed in the more traditional expository styles. Finally, drama exploits the interplay of intellect and emotion in school settings where all too typically the former is rewarded and the latter is ignored.

Lee and I take great pride in the quality and imaginativeness of this work. If Joe, Laura, and Carole think of us as parents of this work, we are deeply honored. Like all good parents, we will take no credit for the wonderful accomplishments of our children. Of course, we would just as soon not be blamed for their shortcomings, either. (We haven't seen any in this collection, mind you.) And since the editors are all productive and prolific teacher educators, we look forward to hearing from the grandchildren in due time.

Judy Shulman, *Institute for Case Development WestEd*
Lee S. Shulman, *Carnegie Foundation for the Advancement of Teaching*

Acknowledgments

This book would not have been possible without the work of Judith and Lee Shulman, who first introduced us to case-based teaching, and Jean Clandinin, who writes about the incredible potential of teacher narratives. We never would have started this project in the first place if they had not carefully laid some firm stepping-stones before us.

Our universities have encouraged us both financially and professionally. We wish to thank the University of Alberta for providing funds from the Support for the Advancement of Scholarship Fund, Faculty of Education, which enabled practicing teachers to gather and write case responses, as well as a research assistant during the final stages of this project. Diane Conrad, a graduate student of Joe's, spent many hours revising earlier drafts and assisted in keeping the many submissions organized. Her helping hand is embedded throughout this text. The University of Arizona was particularly generous by providing funds for the duplication and mailing of early drafts to colleagues worldwide. The University of Victoria supported our efforts through work-study aid as well as departmental assistance.

Critical to this collection were the classroom teachers who read cases and wrote responses. In generously sharing their insights, these teachers enriched this work through their perspectives and experiences. Several of our drama education colleagues have also been a part of this work from the very beginning. Their feedback on earlier drafts of the book and their insights into its potential have been invaluable. More recently, we have received incredible support and encouragement from our international colleagues and are forever grateful.

Over the past six years we have been fortunate to work with hundreds of drama education majors and minors at our three universities. During this time, we have used collections of case narratives as a teaching tool, learning along with our students. Although only eighteen cases and student responses appear here, those eighteen represent all the students who have joined us in learning to teach. This book literally could not have been possible without them—they were both the impetus and the benefactors of our work.

The following are those who have written case studies, student teacher responses, and/or practicing teaching responses: Stephanie Adams, Ellen Arrand, Glenys Berry, Brian Billo, George Blazek, Sue Carberry, Diane Conrad, Jen Craig, Deb Ebling, Doug Ellis, Peter Fenton, Regan Gramlich, Judy Harrison, Jennifer Jensen, Rick Kenney, Kris Kissell, Emil Lamanda, Erin Lawley, Jackie MacDonald, Morgan McLeod, Darrell Marko, Jennifer O'Ryan, Ted Osborne, Deanna Ozburn, Bali Panaser, Mary Ellen Perley, Christine Roberts, Mark Samuel, Merry Saver, Kent Sorensen, Elena Soreham, Peter Spencer, Melody Starman-Moon, Pat Stevenson, Wendy Jo Strom, Lee Stubbs, Paola Unger, Amy Lynn Vero, Tomo Vranjes, Cathleen With.

Lastly, we each owe so much to one another.

Introduction

Other people's stories—those are the ones I crave . . . Not the stories I already know, but the ones I haven't heard yet. The ones that will show me a way out of here. The point is not to emulate others' lives or usurp their wardrobes. The point is to find sense.

—Kingsolver, *High Tide in Tucson*

LET'S GATHER 'ROUND THE FIRESIDE AND TELL STORIES

Joe Norris tells this story:

I was assigned as a site supervisor for a group of student teachers in a junior high where I was expected to "blend in." I wandered the school on a daily basis and, while I was known to the staff and student teachers, the students did not know my role nor did they know that I had twelve years of junior high teaching experience. For them I was a visitor. My reputation did not precede me.

Because I had always enjoyed the challenge of teaching adolescents, I accepted when a teacher asked for someone to cover for her. I knew that the class was a difficult one and keeping the lid on would be a challenge. The students met my expectations. At the beginning of the class I introduced myself and informed them of their assignment.

While there was some chatter and some students were off-task, I was especially concerned by the strange behavior from a group of males. As they pretended to work, they were smiling at one another and running their hands through their own hair. I finally caught on. They were testing me, making fun of my baldness. They were seeing if I was savvy enough to catch on and what I might do in response.

My blood boiled; I was tempted to yell that they were disrespectful. I wanted to kick out the ringleader. Wrong! I'd be putting him in the hall where he wanted to be and I knew that, inevitably, his friends would soon follow. Besides, the act was ambiguous enough to get us into a useless argument. I just didn't want to go there. My mind raced; twelve years had not prepared me for this. I was not a recognized staff member and my authority was zilch. What could I do?

I recalled an anecdote from *Stories of Teaching* (Parsons and Beauchamp 1990) that told of a class of students who, on cue, all dropped their books on the floor. They landed with a resounding thud, thus leaving the novice teacher perplexed. Her response, however, was unique and effective. She walked over to her desk, dropped her books on the floor and said, "I'm sorry, I'm late." Then she picked up the books and resumed the lesson. From this, I found a parallel that I could use in my situation.

I waited for the next person to brush his hair. Luckily, it was the suspected ringleader. As he brushed his hair, I looked him straight in the eye and stroked my beard. By this action I let them know that I considered them bald too. They laughed and we got reasonably back to task.

The next day in the hall, I met the ringleader, who promptly brushed his hair, and I responded by stroking my beard. We had developed a friendly, stylized "handshake."

Listening to the stories of others is not only an opportunity to share in their adventures but an opportunity to build on their experiences (Barone 1990). As we read the stories of others, we resonate with certain parts, making them our own, and in so doing learn vicariously through their experiences (Donmoyer 1990). But the fireside offers more than just learning from listening to others' stories; we also learn by telling our own. Clandinin et al. (1993) point out how this is particularly true for teachers: "As we listen to each other's stories and [tell] our own we learn to make sense of our teaching practices as expressions of our personal practical knowledge" (1).

Our storytelling, then, is a form of reflective practice; it assists us in reexamining past events. When we frame and structure a previously lived event, the meaning of the event can change (Cell 1984). Our audiences can act as catalysts for us. Without their knowing it, they have influenced the manner in which we make meaning. Consequently, after the recounting of an event, we understand it differently. We begin to recognize that all stories are "true fictions" (Denzin 1989).

Our audience, however, can be more than a passive catalyst. Many times our stories are told in conversation. People ask questions, challenge assumptions, give opinions, and tell similar stories of their own. Through conversation and the juxtaposition of our stories with others, our stories are again reshaped. The experience is enriched when the stories both affirm and question our assumptions.

Preservice drama teachers who have used these narrative cases appreciated the opportunity to think through scenarios in the luxury of a classroom full of peers before experiencing them firsthand in their own classrooms. Many claimed that reading and discussing cases enabled them to contextualize their learning and to move from theory to practice. Experienced drama teachers have also found the book valuable. When they read the cases, they began to relive many of their own stories, both questioning and affirming their beliefs and practices. Some remembered their own beginnings, empathizing with the student teachers. The case narratives enabled drama teacher educators to make closer contact with the field. Based upon these student teacher-written narratives, they modified their classes in response to the insights gained from the cases.

THE BIRTH OF THIS BOOK

"What would you do if . . ." is a common question from our drama education students. We found that we could seldom answer the question directly because each situation is contextual; each teacher act is informed by a large set of particulars, with the answer often embedded in the margins. Sometimes we responded with a story of a similar event and an explanation of what we did. But we wanted more than "our" stories. We believe that there is no single good way to teach; what may work successfully for one teacher might not work as well for another. As Noddings (1984) suggests, a teacher's responsibility is to give students possibilities from many perspectives, of which the teacher's is but one. Our stories, while valuable, were mostly from a singular perspective.

Education texts also fell short. While they provided perspectives different from our own, they were not drama-specific. Students in drama classes are seldom in desks and the degree of participation and group work is much greater than is typically found in classrooms. Drama is a place where teachers and students work collaboratively in many creative ventures. We know that the establishment of a healthy classroom climate varies with the context.

Case-based teaching (L. Shulman 1993) provided us with a possible methodology. Case studies could address many "What if . . ." questions. "Case-based teaching provides teachers with opportunities to analyze situations and make judgments in the messy world of practice, where principles often appear to conflict with one another and no simple solution is possible" (J. Shulman 1992, xiv).

Joe began by having his students write reflections of their peer teaching and read examples of cases from *Diversity in the Classroom: A Casebook for Teachers and Teacher Educators* (Shulman and Mesa-Bains 1993). His initial intention was to have them reflect on their practicum through case writing. This would create a stronger transition from university classrooms to the practicum and back again. Because many students wrote strong cases, Joe requested permission to use their cases in subsequent years and to share them with colleagues. (See Appendix C for a copy of the permission form.) The cases would be used not only to discuss teaching issues but also to serve as exemplars of reflective writing.

At the same time, Laura McCammon was using case writing and case-based teaching with her secondary education students at East Tennessee State University. When she began teaching drama/theatre education at the University of Arizona in 1995, she actually organized her drama methods class around Joe's collection, using the cases to explore specific class topics.

While Joe and Laura were beginning to explore case-based teaching, Carole Miller was faced with a dilemma. The program at the University of Victoria was changing; students no longer would connect their fall methods course work with a practicum in the same semester. They would student teach the following term, and she needed a methodology that could contextualize the theoretical precepts of her teaching. The student teacher-written cases provided the necessary material to bridge theory and practice. Her students wrote responses to the cases and used them to examine their own understandings and beliefs.

There are eighteen case narratives in this present collection written by student teachers from the University of Alberta, the University of Arizona, and the University of Victoria. The stories typically represent the concerns of beginning teachers: planning lessons, knowing students as individuals and members of a group, establishing classroom climate, understanding the place of drama within the school community, and expecting the unexpected. Students from these three universities also wrote the student teacher responses that follow each case, and drama teachers from the Edmonton, Tucson, and Victoria areas, most of whom served as cooperating teachers, wrote the teacher responses. We wrote the extensions that appear with each case narrative.

As we edited the cases, we tried to use consistent terminology throughout. We referred to student teaching as "practicum" and call the classroom teacher who was mentoring the student teacher the "cooperating teacher." We used the Canadian references to secondary grade levels—grade 8, grade 9, etc.

Drama is a social art form that demands taking multiple perspectives. We have used this philosophical underpinning to structure our book. Consequently it is a compilation of many voices, each with his or her own unique understanding of what it means to teach drama. Because good stories and case narratives beget other stories, we invite you to add your stories to better understand what it means to teach.

USING THE BOOK

Our intention in compiling this book is to produce an open text. The collection of cases, responses, and extensions is provided as one tool to assist those who wish to utilize this process in their own professional development. In our classrooms we use them to stimulate reflection and to initiate discussion. As you use this book, we hope that your emergent meanings will take precedence over the meanings provided within.

We do, however, have one caveat: We ask readers to treat all of the case narratives and responses with respect and dignity. The writers bravely consented to have their stories made public so that others could learn from them. Unlike the stories told face to face at a party, the readers and writers do not know one another and therefore cannot negotiate the emergent meanings. Read, then, as you would like your own struggles to be read.

When Carole's students respond to a case, she suggests that they treat the case writer as "every teacher" and think about possibilities, rather than placing blame or stating what the student teacher should have done. She asks them to "walk in another's shoes" and to consider the reasons that the writer might have taken a particular course of action. The students imagine, "If this were me, what would I do?", applying their analysis to their own understanding and future practice.

READING THE CASES AND RESPONSES

The following may assist you in getting started:

- Assign one specific case with accompanying responses, along with questions to consider, for discussion in class.
- Read the cases without referring to the responses and use the responses in subsequent discussions.
- Have your students read the entire collection and form small groups to discuss cases/common topics of their choice.
- Build a role-playing exercise based on a situation drawn from a case.

- Begin by reading—rather than writing—case narratives. This will provide you with a variety of exemplars of both form and content. From there, your own cases will flow.

WRITING RESPONSES

Reflective writing is an art. One has to synthesize the myriad of experiences into relevant and meaningful pieces by stepping back to look from a different place; an experience-far perspective (Geertz 1974). Reflective writing not only tells a story but searches for meaning in its telling. While rewarding for many of us, this way of writing is unfamiliar. Consequently, it is a skill that needs to be honed and practiced. Thus, the writing of a response, besides an end in itself, becomes a preparation for the writing of a case.

Joe begins with an activity that he designed to help his students write journals. He starts by having the class sit in a circle and listen to Harry Chapin's (1978) "Flowers Are Red." Chapin's song describes a little boy who wants to use all colors of the rainbow to paint flowers but is told by his teacher that flowers are red and there's no need to see them any other way. The teacher finally forces the little boy to see flowers her way. Once the song ends, Joe asks his students to write nonstop for five minutes, responding to the song. He instructs them to write continuously, not to censor. Chapin's lyrics are strong enough to get a good response from most. We call this stage "describe."

The next stage is called "analyze." He asks the students' permission to pass their writing to the person on the left, careful to point out that they have the right to dissent if they do not wish to share their writing. Most, however, are comfortable and pass their writing on. The next person is instructed to read the piece and respond by uncovering the issues in the piece and making connections to educational theory and the teaching of drama. Those who have chosen not to share are asked to analyze it for themselves.

The final stage is called "apply." For a second time the writing is passed to the left. The third person is instructed to read both pieces and then write concretely about what she or he might do to extend these insights into practice. This writing could be in the form of a lesson plan, a list of teacher activities, or a general set of statements on the teacher's stance.

This preliminary activity of "describe, analyze, and apply" is used to structure the writing of the cases and responses. Joe, however, is quick to point out that the final written piece need not be as linear as the original exercise but all of the elements should be included. Each of us has taken aspects of the others' work and created strong hybrids for teaching reflective writing. Writing responses to cases is part of the process and a valuable activity in itself. (See Appendix B for a copy of the case response assignment.)

WRITING CASES

> Telling our stories brings order to our experience, and helps us to view our lives both subjectively and objectively at the same time. (Atkinson 1995, 6–7)

If the foundation that is suggested above is well-laid, the transition to writing a case narrative is a natural next step. But finding that case is not as easy. We need a form of patience and vigilance, during which time we are ever watchful. While the classroom is full of opportunities to find a case, the true intent of the assignment is not the writing of a case narrative; rather, the case narrative is a tool to assist one in better understanding his or her practice. The case emerges from the question "What do I want to better understand?" (See Appendix A for a copy of the case study assignment.)

We recommend a case narrative journal as a tool to assist one in this search/journey. We suggest that you keep a daily list—and we do mean list—of events, questions, and concerns. This provides a beginning from which a case can grow. Often people initially believe that only significant events are worth listing. This process is like mining; you go through a lot of slag before you find a gem. However, when discovered, the light of the gem makes the drudgery of mining worthwhile.

When Laura's student teachers begin writing their case narratives, she first asks them to discuss possible topics, drawn from their journals. During seminars they share their stories with their peers for feedback. When they write the case, she advises them to tell the story as completely as possible, remembering to include all the background information that a reader might need to understand the context of the case. She advises them to write only what they have observed, not to write what they assume others think. For example, it would not be appropriate for a case writer to say, "She deliberately tried to sabotage my lesson," because the writer has no way of knowing a student's state of mind. It would be more accurate to say, "Instead of participating in the warm-up, the student began to talk to a friend about a movie they had both seen." Then Laura asks the students to step back in order to distance themselves from the case before analyzing events and applying what they have learned to future practice. When time permits, the student teachers give her a rough draft of their case for feedback before submitting their final copy.

EXTENSIONS

The cases raise many relevant issues. We have found that we always have more material to cover than class time permits. We have focused on some of these issues through the suggested activities and extension questions, but we encourage you to discover others. The extensions also refer you to other pertinent literature. Please feel free to choose and adapt them to meet your needs.

ETHICS

As readers we have been privileged to share the stories of students and teachers and the meanings they give to their experiences. With this privilege comes responsibility. We ask that you discuss the cases with the respect that their writers deserve. This does not mean that you won't question or critique; but remember that each writer is presenting only one small part of her or his continuing quest of becoming a teacher. Consequently, we have chosen to acknowledge all of the contributors together rather than list each individually with his or her case or response. In this way, we recognize them yet maintain anonymity. Each author has used pseudonyms in his or her story and we have removed specific references that could identify a particular context to ensure that all other parties remain anonymous.

AN INVITATION

If every story begs another, we hope that these are just the beginning. We invite you to read and write on.

1

Planning Lessons

BRIDGING THE GAP: DRAMA VS. ACTING WITH COMBINED GRADE LEVELS

This case explores the process versus product dilemma in a high school drama class in which students of various ages and drama experience are placed together.

How do you teach a drama class composed of students from grades 9, 10, 11, and 12—all working at different levels of experience and expertise? That was the challenge facing me as I looked at the enrollment list for the class I was to teach. The list included seven students in grade 9 drama, ten students in grade 10 drama, nine students in Acting 11, and four students in Acting 12. The rationale was that combining various grade levels in one block of drama made it feasible to add that class to the schedule. But if, for example, it were just a grade 9/10 class, there would not have been enough students participating to offer the course at that time.

On the first day of class, the grade 9 students, still fresh from middle school, looked apprehensively at the older, more vocal students. The seniors looked doubtfully at the rest of the class and at the student teacher before them. I announced that we had a special challenge with this wide range in experience—everyone would have to work together, with the older, more experienced students serving as role models.

Within the first two weeks, many of the seniors had shifted to a different class, leaving four students enrolled in Acting 11, six in grade 10, and seven in grade 9. We started with basic trust- and team-building activities, and the students—mostly young women—came together well. There was cooperation and focus and I was very pleased with their progress.

My greatest challenge with the group was finding the "right pitch" for the work we undertook. I tried different kinds of role drama work along with writing and staging scenes around the theme of family

1

conflict. However, the older students' drama journals revealed that, while they were enjoying the class, some felt they had already covered the basics in previous years and weren't learning much. I challenged them to deepen the quality of their work.

When we did a unit on storytelling and story theatre, which culminated in presentations of the fable *Two Crows* (cited in Lundy and Booth 1983), most of the work was relatively superficial. Many of the younger students voiced this attitude: "How can we take this stuff seriously? Let us work on a script about people." I pointed out that the actor's first tool is imagination and explained how Disney films deal with important themes using animal characters and animation. Our discussion seemed to help them appreciate this kind of work, but as a neophyte teacher I was constantly wondering if the work was "appropriate" for the group.

It was clear to me that most of them had only scratched the surface of the possibilities inherent in the script. I judged that I needed to push them further in my coaching as they worked on projects.

Drawing on ideas from my cooperating teacher, I explained that a drama teacher cannot drag a student into work that reflects a greater complexity, more layers, or more attention to detail. The teacher can only provide an environment in which the student may choose to take on the challenge for him- or herself—moving beyond the comfortable and the superficial. I worried that I was beginning to sound like a broken record.

Because I was generally pleased with the quality of work in the first six weeks, I agreed that we would work toward the rehearsal and performance of scenes from plays. This seemed to be the goal of many students. They wanted the challenge of characters and scripts, not the improvisation-based role work that I felt was more appropriate for a class that was mostly grade 9/10.

I was hesitant about rushing into scene work without providing an adequate base in focus, improvisation, characterization, and range in their "emotional palette" through various exercises and activities. Yet the senior students were ready, and several of the grade 9 and 10 students were doing excellent work. I wanted to challenge them and also move in a direction that would be fulfilling for them.

In the second half of my practicum, I had the students choose a play or novel, then write and deliver a monologue as one of its characters. I monitored the choices and the writing process, offering encouragement and suggestions. I could tell that some students were going to do very well with the assignment, but for others, their lack of writing experience or their choice of novel was getting in the way.

When the time for performance came, half the class was ready and the work was quite good. The other half, including one Acting 11 student, was ill-prepared. For some, the writing had taken too long and they had not allowed enough time to memorize their scripts, in spite of my time guidelines. One student never performed; she had changed her source text midway and had no script to submit.

I felt as though I had failed those students in a major way. In seeking to move them through to scene work, had I assumed too much and missed some basic steps? I realize now that the reading, synthesizing, writing, and rehearsing involved in this kind of project was quite complex. It was very demanding for students with poor English skills, for those who were already overloaded with work in the school play, and for those who were only taking drama because of the fine arts requirement in the curriculum. When I commented on the wide range in the quality of work and levels of commitment to the process, I was criticized by two students for "picking on them," although I had not singled out anyone in particular. It's in times like these that a student teacher wonders if she or he is taking the class in the right direction.

We moved into some fun and funny improvisation work that gave several of the students who hadn't done well with their monologues the opportunity to demonstrate their improvisation and comedy skills. Next, I wanted to clarify the concepts of character motivation and objectives through some role improvisation based around a short scene. This would help lay the foundation before we moved on to text work.

Evidently, however, I hadn't made my purpose and direction clear enough. On the second day, I met with a kind of mini-revolution, a work stoppage. Several students were fed up with working on improvisation that didn't progress to a final product and the rest of the class generally agreed with them. I repeated that I was looking to deepen the quality of their work, but when I got more resistance I asked, "Where do we go from here?" When they said they wanted scenes for groups of four or five, I answered that that was what we were moving toward. The next day I brought in scenes from *Steel Magnolias* and *Lost in Yonkers*. They promptly got to work.

During this process, one group of five young women working on a scene from *Steel Magnolias* came to a point of crisis and split into two groups. Three of them wanted to do a really good job and put in extra rehearsal time. It was clear that the other two were dragging them down with their lackadaisical attitude and lack of interest in progressing beyond the minimum effort.

In the end, most of the groups showed relatively good work, and the work from the Acting 11 students was excellent. The class enjoyed the scene work and moved on to other "deepening" activities when my cooperating teacher took over the class at the end of my practicum.

I still wrestle with the choices I made along the way. Was I clear enough in outlining my expectations? I got the impression that some students got tired of me always asking them to go deeper into the work, beyond the surface, into the layers where character work becomes richer and more three-dimensional.

Students like to work on scenes; there is safety in the written text and character types they already know how to "do," or in small parts that require little memorization. Scene work can be a wonderful challenge for aspiring thespians, yet the work can easily remain superficial, perpetuating bad acting habits unless the teacher is willing to work the scenes further—in effect, directing with the rest of the class watching.

The main challenge seems to be getting the balance right between drama work that is process-oriented and acting work that is performance-driven. Students must understand how interrelated the two are, how an actor draws on craft that comes through hard work. They need the opportunity for both kinds of experience because both are important. But unless the drama work is constantly compelling— and thus more demanding for the drama teacher!—students will probably opt for scene work, for "putting on a little show" that will develop certain skills, but which can sometimes miss the heart of drama completely. When classes involve students at very different grade or experience levels, this challenge is all the more complex.

A Student Teacher's Response: Nurturing Growth

The student teacher in this case was challenged by a class of combined grade levels—grade 9/10 and Acting 11/12. I admire how the teacher addressed the issue head-on with the students and had a discussion acknowledging the "special challenge" of the task ahead for everyone. This seems like such a small, but still difficult, thing to do; it takes an honest teacher to admit that to the class. With this small beginning step, this teacher has shown me that she or he is willing to risk showing a tiny bit of fear and at the same time is asking for the help and engagement of the collective group. The teacher is an inch closer to establishing trust.

The beginning of the class was the most difficult for this teacher.

The teacher states that the hardest task was "finding the 'right pitch.' " I think that the teacher's theme idea on family conflict was a good one because it is ageless and can be explored by all students, regardless of drama experience. The students had a hard time getting into *Two Crows*; the younger students scoffed at the crow/human symbolism, and the older students quietly resisted. The teacher talked with the students about imagination and the emotional similarities of animated or animal characters in Disney films, animal stories, and fables. Because they responded well to this discussion the teacher decided he or she was going to need to push the students further. The teacher talked about the choices in drama and how drama is about working on layers of meaning, complexity, attention to detail, and emotional depth. He or she stressed to the students that the onus was on them to make that choice. He or she provided the opportunity and the leadership, but they ultimately had to choose to take the risk.

The students worked steadfastly on their family conflict themes and the teacher decided afterward, to respond to their desire to do short acting scenes. The teacher was concerned about the students' foundations at this point: Did they have enough background in focus or improvisation?

I think that this teacher's concerns were dead-on, and what she or he said about commitment and choice was accurate. How do you provide an energized, safe, and respectful space to foster students' engagement? This case is a brilliant example of how you can plant the seeds for drama to grow, but sometimes you have to sit back and watch for the tiny green shoot and hope for bright sunlight.

I think that this is a case of doing all that you can as a drama teacher: listening to the students' desires, talking with the cooperating teacher, utilizing strategies, testing limits, pushing tasks, expecting meaning, wanting quality of depth, but still seeing occasions of superficiality in the students' work. As this teacher learns, the choice lies in the heart of the learner. After all is said and done, the teacher must let go and accept that meaningful growth is not always marked by age, level, or experience—some seeds find their way through the soil by groping blindly until the desire for light forces them through.

A Teacher's Response: Finding the Right Balance

This case accentuates two dilemmas facing many drama teachers today. The teacher's opening question is one I face every year lately: How do you teach a drama class composed of students from various grade levels? Mixed drama classes are now the norm in many rural schools. With an increasingly crowded program of studies, drama programs are being "squeezed" and timetables adjusted so that students can "fit" drama into their course selections for the year. Like me, the student teacher in "Bridging the Gap" was faced with the enigmatic challenge of "finding the 'right pitch'" for the work he or she undertook with a mixed drama class.

In finding the right pitch, how does one create a successful learning environment? How can a teacher introduce those students with little or no drama experience to drama process work that is "at their level," while at the same time challenging those students with considerably more experience to "deepen the quality of their drama work"?

The second dilemma facing the teacher in "Bridging the Gap" was the dichotomy between process (drama) work and product (theatre) work. How does a teacher balance drama games, activities, and improvisations used to develop skills with the demand by students for "the play"? Ironically, one is often faced with just the opposite problem— students who would rather "play" than "work" on textual materials.

This case reveals some of the situations facing many drama teachers in the field today. How much give-and-take should there be between the teacher's goals and the interests and wants of the students in the class? In her or his conclusion, the student teacher reflects on the fears that she or he may have "failed" the students. Was the teacher moving them too fast, missing key steps, possibly giving them material that was too demanding? Was she or he "taking the class in the right direction"? The dilemma the teacher was faced with in finding the right pitch was trying to balance his or her vision with the conflicting desires of the students. Because of the composition of the combined class and the preconceptions the students had of "serious" drama work, the teacher was caught in a tricky balancing act.

The "gap" the teacher tries to bridge is one I face every year. The following are a few keys to successfully coping that I find work for me.

1. A clearly articulated "continuum" that ensures that process and product are in as much balance as possible. Students must come to appreciate that process work is a means of "deepening the quality of their work." A logical continuum will push students to "go deeper" in their drama explorations and eventually will manifest itself in a higher-quality product.
2. Use the mixed bag of talents and experience you end up with in a combined class in such a way as to achieve the objectives you wish to achieve. Experienced students are wonderful mentors for younger drama students—they act so well as leaders, directors,

critics, facilitators, etc. The key is in finding meaningful ways to use these students to help the teacher achieve a positive classroom atmosphere, while providing challenges for them.

In this case, the cooperating teacher wisely gave the teacher under her or his care the freedom to struggle in finding the right pitch with this particular class. However, he or she may have been wise in suggesting to the student teacher that the experienced students may be used in leadership roles in some of the activities or projects undertaken.

This case certainly challenged me to reflect upon my own teaching practice and on the dilemmas I face each year with my mixed classes. Finding that balance is the key.

The student teacher's response was very reassuring and contains a truth that I hope many who become drama teachers will take to heart. The seeds image is so very true. Yes, sometimes we need to be patient in accepting the fact that the "choice lies within the heart of the learner." We are certainly reminded that in our eagerness for confirmation that what we are doing is "right," we must not expect instant success. Growth is something slow, "not always marked by age, level, or experience." What a great reassurance in a world of teaching that is often so filled with doubts in trying to find the right pitch!

Extensions

1. How can we help students to move from a superficial to an in-depth drama experience? What is the teacher's responsibility toward achieving an in-depth experience? The students'? Take a short scene that you might teach and plan a few drama activities that could help students enrich their work. See *Structuring Drama Work* (Neelands 1990), *Starting with Scripts* (Kempe 1997), *Drama Sampler* (Kempe 1994) for suggestions.
2. Many classes have students with a wide range of skills. Make a list of skills that you would consider basic and create an orientation unit that provides students with experiences to learn these skills.
3. In this class the student teacher had a wide range—13/14-year-olds to 17/18-year-olds. What do you know about the developmental level of adolescents these ages that you would have to take into consideration if you were planning for a class this diverse?
4. Some of the students were uncomfortable creating a story drama from *Two Crows* because it was an unfamiliar tale. What other kinds of stories might the student teacher have chosen for these

students to work with? What value might there have been in giving several stories to choose from?
5. This case suggests that process work should precede product.
Explain if you agree or disagree. What kinds of experiences can a
teacher provide to enable students to discover for themselves the
value of process work?
6. The student teacher response suggests that sometimes you have
to leave students alone and let them find their own way. How do
you respond to this statement?
7. What value is there in expecting students to give all activities a
try? In *Drama Guidelines* (1976) Cecily O'Neill and her colleagues
state that the functions of a drama teacher include challenging,
arousing interest, giving confidence, coordinating achievement,
and encouraging reflection. They also, however, note that the
drama teacher must sometimes "make anxious" (9). What is your
understanding of these functions?

RHUBARB, RHUBARB, RHUBARB

This student teacher encounters resistance to the use of drama in an English class.

During my practicum I worked harder than I have at any other time
in my life. This hard work has rewarded me with many great experiences in both drama and English classrooms. I also know that teaching is not all sunshine and light. Lessons have fizzled, and students
have stared blankly at me after I have explained an activity with what
I thought was erudite clarity.

Needless to say, this practicum has allowed me to develop my skills
as a speaker, an explainer, and a listener. I now know that it is important for a teacher to listen to the tone and mood of his or her students in the classroom and to adjust his or her planned activities
accordingly. Let me relate one particular instance when I tried to
introduce a drama activity in an English classroom.

I was teaching a grade 12 English class of thirty students. We had
just finished a unit on short stories and I was going to introduce the
next unit of study, the novel *The Apprenticeship of Duddy Kravitz* by
Mordecai Richler (1959). This unit would proceed over three and a
half weeks, and I was confident in my lesson plans and my knowledge
of the novel. What better way to introduce a novel filled with such
vivid characters than to give my students the opportunity to build
some characters of their own, I thought.

My cooperating teacher was not particularly supportive of using drama in the English classroom, especially at a grade 12 level. However, this was still early in the term and would not interfere with the more academic preparation for governmental examinations, so she said I could "take a stab at it."

Mistake number one: It was still early in the term, and my students were not yet used to me. They liked me, and as a result, they were willing to give me the benefit of the doubt and give this "weird drama thing" a shot. However, I had not fully earned their trust, and these very auditory learners found it difficult to leave the safety of their desks.

Mistake number two: I asked them to involve themselves in a role-playing activity right after I handed back a test on the short story unit. Most of the students performed very poorly on this test and were very vocal about their poor marks and what they saw as an unfair test.

The test was closure to a peer teaching activity, for which each group of students in the class was responsible for presenting and explaining the elements of one of the following short story terms: plot, character, theme, setting, humor, emotion. One group of students wrote the test based on the members' notes from these presentations. Not only did the students write the test themselves, but they had to administer it, mark it, and adjust the marks if there was a discrepancy. The rest of the class found many discrepancies and was grumbling loudly to the group of students who had written the test.

For a moment, I looked at the situation from outside myself, and the grumbling reminded me of when I murmured "Rhubarb, rhubarb, rhubarb . . ." on stage to suggest a crowd scene in a university theatre production.

Before the grumbling progressed into an all-out war, I put a stop to the review of the test and placated the class as best as I could. I sent the test writers off to reassess some of their questions most under fire and proceeded to introduce the role-playing activity.

Mistake number three: I asked the students to leave their desks and move to the front of the room, and then I explained the "Famous People" role drama and its connection to the novel, which I knew was solid and clear. The novel is about one young man's pursuit of success and recognition. Each student was to think of someone famous and successful in his or her field of specialty. The students could choose living or deceased actors, musicians, sports figures, politicians, academics, etc.

Once they had someone in mind, they were to imagine how that person moved and spoke and then they were to imagine that they were all at a convention of famous people. Each person was to greet at least three other people in role as his or her famous character. The objective was to find out who those other famous people were without actually asking them their names. The way to probe for the others' identities was to ask questions.

So the connection was clear, but the activity itself was too risky to fully engage the class. They stood very close to one another; there was a lot of nervous laughter, and they worked to achieve their objective as quickly as possible so they could return to their seats. Only two students were actually in role, and they were from my Acting 12 class.

In retrospect, I should have done this activity later on in the unit when the class was more relaxed with me and with one another. The activity would have meant more to the students when they had more background and experience with the novel. In place of this activity, I could have assigned a short story that had a connection to the theme or content of the novel to read in class, or I could have handed out the novel and done some prediction and anticipation exercises with the class.

I could have adapted this activity so that the students could have participated from their desks or asked them to write a short "Who Am I?" piece of creative writing. Alternatively, I could have done the activity but provided more preparation and lead-up to the role play, and therefore ease my students into it instead of expecting them to jump in, inexperienced and unsure. Above all, I should have listened to the tone of the class as a whole, anticipating their needs.

From this experience, I have learned to slow down and ride alongside my students, sending out feelers for which activities might be appropriate. If their needs require something other than the activity I have planned, I have to have an alternative prepared or even ask the students for their suggestions.

My seniors helped me use drama in the classroom later on in the novel unit. This time I involved them in a low-risk tableau exercise. We picked a scene from the novel and sculpted it, and then students wrote from the point of view of a character of their choice from the living picture that they had created. Drama in my English classroom will work as long as I continue to listen to my students.

A Student Teacher's Response: When a Class Gives You Rhubarb, Add Sugar and Make a Pie

This case is about what happened when the student teacher tried to use drama in the English classroom. The students were not yet used to the student teacher, and there was a lack of trust among the members of the class. The class was not eased into role play but was expected to just jump in and go for it.

According to the author, one of the first mistakes was that it was early in the term and the students were not yet used to the student teacher. They may have liked her or him, but there was no real trust established, which is critical when working in the medium of drama. In order for any learning and risk taking to occur in drama, there must be a feeling of security and openness in the classroom. These feelings were obviously missing from this class.

There were a few other minor factors that were detrimental to the success of this lesson. One of these was the timing in handing back tests on which students had performed poorly. The teacher did this immediately before introducing the role drama. Of course the students would be uncomfortable. They had just had a minor bomb dropped in their laps, and they were expected to put it aside and move on into unfamiliar territory. Not a good way to start! Finally, the students had been thrown into the deep end and were expected to swim. You must start by introducing the concept and slowly easing them into it, much like any work in drama, especially role play.

In this case the student teacher was aware of all of the factors that hindered the role play. He or she was able to adjust his or her approach and try again later in the course. It was great that the teacher was able to see these mistakes and correct them. In the future, students of this particular class might be more willing to do drama, whereas if the student teacher had given up on using drama in the English classroom, the students may never have experienced the satisfaction and magic that is created when using drama to learn.

In reading this case, I have learned that in order to use drama in the classroom the teacher must create a safe environment and prepare the students for working with role drama. Easing the students in with small, low-risk activities can help make the students feel comfortable about using drama. I am going to use drama in my English classes, but I will be very aware of how I go about doing it, especially after reading this case.

A Teacher's Response: Easy Does It

In this case the student teacher has clearly reflected on the class and has pointed out the mistakes she or he thought she or he made. Reflection on the day's activities is a major part of the teaching process. It is through honest reflection that the teacher is able to access what works and what needs adjustment. It is important to listen to the tone of the class and be responsive to the mood of the students. Whenever a teacher is thinking of trying something new, it is necessary to remember how we ourselves feel when faced with something new. Gently does it. Allow time for adjustment to the new ideas.

Teachers must take into account that the moment they determine will be the beginning of something new might not be the "right time" for the students. It is important to set up the environment for a new approach. This requires building trust with the students first by slowly introducing the methods. The teacher was already aware that the students were predisposed to auditory learning, i.e. sitting in desks. This should signal a need to offer a slow entrance into the drama methods, perhaps by allowing students to sit and listen first. In the case outlined the students did not have the requisite trust in place, nor was the moment right for the introduction of the idea. Again, the teacher was aware of this, because he or she pointed out that he or she introduced the "new" right after returning marked work. This grading was fraught with consternation on the part of several class members and thus the mood was not conducive to trying something new and possibly threatening. Furthermore, not everyone was going to be in the class for this new work, potentially creating new challenges for the next class.

It is important to bring closure to one activity before moving on to another, especially if the next activity is something new. In the student teaching situation it is important to have the cooperating teacher's support. In this case that support did not seem to be there. So the student teacher was that much more "at risk" with this new idea of drama in English. It is hard to say what to do in such a situation. Should one soldier on, convinced of the pedagogical soundness, or defer because of a lack of emotional support?

It is also important for a teacher to be aware of the nature of peer evaluation. In this situation, the teacher needed to look at the material that had been marked before returning it. This step might have been proactive in dealing with the disgruntled feelings of the class.

In developing trust, the teacher could have played some games to set up trust building as well as facilitating a discussion of students' perceptions of drama. This could serve the purpose of getting all ideas and misconceptions out on the table. If a teacher is going to ask students to use a specific strategy, such as hot seating, modeling it for students might give them ideas of how to do it. Not being able to picture how something is played out can often be a barrier to some students.

Leaving the desks was also a problem for the students as they were entering unfamiliar territory. Again, the teacher needs to remember to ease students into the unfamiliar. Perhaps the student teacher could have had the students write about their famous person first, describe this person to a partner, then try to physicalyze the character, then vocalize him or her. All this work could be done in pairs or small groups to increase the feeling of safety.

It is a shame that the teacher felt compelled to abandon the activity. With a slower entry and appropriate timing I believe the integration of drama and English would have proven a rewarding experience for teacher and students alike.

Extensions

1. Students often bring with them certain ideas of how English—or any other subject—should be taught. What kinds of expectations and fears might be raised when the teacher announces in an English class, "We are going to do drama"? Read Warner's (1998) article and make a list of ways in which you can help to ease students into drama work.
2. Imagine that an English teacher has come to you and asked for ideas for doing drama in her or his class. What suggestions would you make?
3. Set up an improvisation that takes place in the teacher's lounge between a teacher who does not think that drama is appropriate, especially in a core subject, and a teacher who believes in drama's potential for learning.

STEEL BAR IN SPOKES LEADS TO A TUMBLE

In this observational situation the methods student describes what can go wrong when students don't treat the improvisational drama with respect.

Recently I had the opportunity to observe three grade 10 and 11 drama classes while they worked on scenes. The grade 11 acting class was just starting a unit on scene work in pairs. The students in the grade 10 advanced class were preparing to present their mime scenes for an audience, and the grade 10 regular class was wrapping up a unit on mime and students were to present their scenes to the class. It was here that I was confronted with how easy it is for students to stick a metal bar into the spokes of the dramatic wheel.

It was a Friday afternoon, the first block after lunch. The last of the mime presentations were wrapped up in the first half of the class, and there were still forty minutes remaining. The teacher had the students perform improvisations in which the actors were to create a situation and establish an activity before finding a way to exit the scene. Some of the students didn't take it seriously at all, affecting the whole feel of the exercise.

During the improvisation, the teacher approached me and asked if I would like to take part in a role drama for the next exercise. I agreed to be in role as an eighty-year-old man who lived next to a park and who was concerned about the noise level. The teacher would be in role as the chairperson of a town meeting called to address my complaints.

The teacher welcomed everyone to the meeting, introduced me, and explained why the meeting was called. The students were quick to take on roles as citizens and started asking questions about me and the noise in the park. Some students sided with me and some opposed my concerns. About five minutes into the drama the metaphoric steel bar was thrust into the spokes. One of the students, in role as a nine-year-old child, accused me of being a dirty old man and hanging around the girls changing room at the swimming pool.

This remark got others going: "Yeah, I saw him there, too!" I felt as though a huge boulder had been dropped on my chest, and my mind scrambled to keep me from sinking. It was at this time that the teacher looked at me and asked if I would like to tell them about the time I was honored for saving children's lives. My mind raced as I improvised the scenario of saving four children from drowning when I was a young man, back in the 1930s. I was really grateful for the quick thinking of the teacher, keeping the drama from getting out of control. The drama wasn't the same after the student accusations, but we did manage to get through it.

I learned from this experience that you really have to prepare your class before you start working with role playing. Everyone must understand the rules and abide by them. These students weren't told enough beforehand, which I believe contributed to the problem.

There were times when I felt the teacher could have stopped the drama in order to refocus the students, but this never occurred. Overall, I feel that there needs to be a lot of preparatory work done before entering into a role drama, especially when the drama could take off in any direction. I felt I was a casualty of this lack of preparation and it didn't have to happen that way.

A Student Teacher's Response: Brush Yourself Off and Keep Pedaling

The student teacher in this case understandably expresses concern because the drama got out of control because of the students' lack of respect for the work. He or she suggested that more preparation is needed before students enter a role drama. I agree that the students need to understand the class rules for drama and that these rules need to be in place at the beginning of the year. As Neelands (1984) states, the students must know that "frivolous responses, jokyness, playing about, thoughtless action, [and] self-indulgent behavior" will not be tolerated. Once a contract is in place with the students, they will accept the teacher stopping the drama to ensure that everyone is comfortable with the direction in which the drama is heading.

I would like to know the manner in which the idea of the "dirty old man" was introduced. If it were meant as a joke, then the idea would have been unacceptable and counter to the contract. However, if it were stated seriously and accepted seriously by other students, then the teacher should have decided with the class if this new idea should be accepted and explored further. What events led up to the accusations? What happened to those children in the 1930s? How did receiving an honor affect this man's life? These ideas could be explored in any number of ways, for example: tableau, improvisation, sitting-down drama, or writing in role.

The student teacher expresses gratitude for the quick thinking of the teacher. Things can get stuck in the wheels of the drama. However, they don't have to be steel bars stuck in the spokes but rather cards that can either make a cool sound or just turn out to be annoying noisemakers.

A Teacher's Response: Clear the Path of Steel Bars and Enjoy the Ride

The best way to avoid the "steel bars" is to clear the path ahead of time. I agree with the student teacher's response that a Friday afternoon drama class can be chaotic unless the teacher maintains a clear focus in the classroom. Chaos may result from the following conditions. First, students have a fresh supply of energy, having just eaten their lunch. Furthermore, most students complement their lunch with an unhealthy supply of candy and pop, leaving them vibrating with frenetic energy when they return to class. Second, students need to talk about what they did—and what they missed—during their lunch break: "Oh my God, Sue broke up with John"; "Aaron ate five hamburgers and threw up"; "We rock 'cause we beat them at two-on-two." If they are not given time to process these important events when they return to class, they will do so during class time, causing disruption or "steel bars" for the teacher to deal with. Finally, the weekend is near and schoolwork may not be a priority. Many people are not at peak performance on Friday afternoon; students are no different—they just want to go home. So, given all of this, how does a teacher ensure that students remain focused on a Friday afternoon? He or she can best accomplish it by offering the students something relevant and meaningful upon which to focus their energy.

I begin almost every drama class with "Talk Time," when we sit in a circle and pass around a talking stick. This enables students to debrief their lunchtime escapades within the construct of a focused classroom activity. As they share stories and update one another on the latest news, much frenetic energy is released. If the energy level is still high and potentially disruptive, a teacher could follow "Talk Time" with a game that involves a lot of movement, such as "Fox and Rabbit," "The Blob," "Fruit Bowl," etc. While these activities may be time-consuming, it is time well spent if all the "steel bars" are removed from your path.

The mime presentations were a good choice on the part of the teacher; presentations are an excellent way to focus a class. Usually students want to do their best because performance requires a lot of work, they do not want to look foolish in front of their peers, and the work will be evaluated. The teacher should have stayed on this path for the remainder of the class rather than shifting gears into an improvisation exercise that had no relevance to the mime scenes.

When a unit concludes with a performance, students feel like they have done the important stuff and anything they do after that is just "busy work." In this case, the teacher's choice to do an unrelated improvisation activity confirmed for the students that the real work was completed. Furthermore, when improvisations are undertaken without a clear focus, self-indulgent behaviour is inevitable. Consequently, a frivolous mood was set with the improvisations, and the role play took on the same quality.

Asking the students to reflect on their mime presentations by facilitating a relaxation exercise would be a more relevant and meaningful follow-up to the exercise. Moreover, most of the learning takes place during reflection as students make sense of their accomplishments. While the students lie down and listen to soft music with their eyes closed, the teacher asks questions such as: "Which performance impressed you the most? What did you like about it? Was it the movement, the use of a mask, or perhaps the meaning of the piece?" Ask students to be specific in determining what made the piece special for them. While the students are in a relaxed state they can be asked to focus on anything that the teacher feels is important. The teacher can then bring the students into a circle to express and share their thoughts. After the sharing session they can record their responses in their journals, which the teacher would then evaluate. Evaluation encourages students to take the work more seriously.

The success of a drama class is contingent upon the teacher anticipating "where the kids are at." Expect that the energy level will be high and unfocused on a Friday afternoon, and prepare an appropriate lesson. Ensure that all the activities are meaningful, relevant, and have a clear focus. Establish what the students' needs are, and allow them to meet those needs within the structure of your drama lesson. If they need to talk, plan a "Talk Time"; if they need to burn off energy, plan an appropriate game. Having students perform on a Friday afternoon is an excellent idea, but stay with the same theme for the duration of the class. Changing gears partway through a class disrupts the continuity of the lesson, and students will react in kind with disruptive behavior. Use reflection to add relevance and meaning to an activity while keeping the energy focused. Finally, evaluate everything. When students know that their work is being evaluated, the quality of their work escalates. In conclusion, knowing that steel bars in your spokes tend to cause tumbles, remember to clear the path ahead of time so that you can enjoy the ride.

Extensions

1. According to the student teacher, one of the cooperating teacher's talents was the ability to think on her or his feet. Some of this is a skill and some of this is the teacher's attitude toward how fixed or how open a particular lesson can/should be. What is your comfort level on the amount of student input into a lesson? What are your boundaries? Make a list of your dos and don'ts for improvisational activities that you would discuss with your students.
2. The student teacher in this case talks about the need to prepare students for role drama. What kinds of skills do students need and what are some activities you could provide so that they will learn those skills?
3. The responding student teacher makes a comment about contracting and stopping the drama. What can be learned if a drama is stopped? What if it's not stopped?
4. When doing in-role work we rely on the imagination of the participants. It works when what is contributed is in the range of plausibility. How will you teach your students to make appropriate choices? What will you do when you believe an inappropriate choice is made?

2

Knowing the Students

ELIMINATING THE CREATURE, EMBRACING THE CREATURE

In the following case, a guided imagery results in distressing several high school students, especially one student who had experienced personal trauma.

As I reached for the script from which I would read, I felt an onslaught of enormous color devour my chest, my hands, and my mouth. An overwhelming sense of possibility had been running free in me for the last twenty-four hours since I was told that I could introduce and work with mask in the grade 12 drama classroom. So, full of energy and anticipation, I arrived early and stayed late for several days to complete the scrumming and wedging of clay that I would need for Friday. Today was Wednesday, and my plan of action seemed a pleasant, if not euphoric, way to lead them into elements of the almighty mask.

I had created a guided-imagery exercise in which the students would relax physically, listen to my voice and directions, and ultimately leave the real world behind for a few moments as they traveled on a journey of connection and spirit. My objective was to have them meet and interact with the person or "thing" that might indeed become the mask they would make that Friday.

As they entered the room, the lights were dimmed and the overhead projected a blue color on the background. The gentle music of Enya was playing, adding to the calm and peaceful atmosphere I thought essential to the guided imagery. As the students found their own spaces and lay down, I noticed some movement and fidgeting, but they gradually relaxed into the exercise.

I knew beforehand that my cooperating teacher needed a specific amount of time to finish an activity; therefore, I was very aware of the time. I was also very conscious of the need to go slowly and allow ample time for the students to imagine and explore the places I described.

I had been careful to incorporate the idea of safety and student control throughout the guided imagery. For example, at the beginning I had them hovering in the room over the floor, then around the school, and finally rising above the school through a hole in the roof. I told them that they had complete control over how high they were at all times. I then had them soaring through the air to various places around the world: a desert, a mountaintop, a huge city. I made it clear that the speed they were going was also entirely in their power. While I tried to eliminate any feelings of harm, I was also trying to give them the freedom to explore numerous possibilities. This is when the creature emerged.

As they were exploring a fantastical environment, where no other person had ever been, I gave them the option of staying there or going back to a more familiar place. Following this, I had them slowly encounter a person, or alien, or *creature* with whom they "instantly felt safe and secure." Despite the safeguard, the initial shock of hearing the word *creature*, or even *alien* for some, destroyed the zone of security I had built around them. Some students saw dark figures, others referred to a feeling of apprehension. Either way I had charted the very territory I was trying to avoid.

During debriefing, my questions uncovered some beautiful, even sacred, experiences for some of the students. One of them, for instance, told us about a glorious beach of blue crystal water, where the student met a "creature" he recognized as elements of his own soul. I thought, "I helped take him to a place of wonder and self-reflection." I was overjoyed as others shared their experiences, some swearing that the existence of the floor below them vanished as their only awareness was of their body.

Then the stories of darkness emerged. In particular, there was one young lady whom I will never forget. She remained for the debriefing but then quickly left. My cooperating teacher told me that Iris had been raped two years earlier and had actually seen the face of her assailant. At that moment the color faded and I felt completely drained. It was obvious that I had assisted in nourishing many minds, but at the same time I had caused anxiety. The pinpointed word was *creature*, and I cursed myself, thinking, "Why wasn't that obvious to me? Why didn't I eliminate the creature?"

I excused myself from the room and scoured the hallways until I found Iris. "I am so sorry . . ." were the words that fell from my mouth, and she sank into my arms crying as I offered her a hug. I asked her if she wanted to talk about it. I have never felt more like a teacher than I did during the next fifteen minutes. Caring contributes to the nucleus of teaching, and on that day, sitting in an abandoned hallway, I made a most vital and caring connection that I will always see as the essence of teaching. How I dreaded that word *creature*—how Iris dreaded it, and yet together we were embracing it.

When we returned to the classroom to collect our things, I discreetly wrote my name and number on a piece of paper and gave it to her. Since she was staying in a halfway house and was new to the school, she felt a bit alienated. She had access to many qualified counselors, and I encouraged her to use them as often as required. My cooperating teacher questioned my decision to give my phone number to Iris, but I honestly felt she needed the act of offering more than she actually needed the number. I strongly believed that it was the right thing for me to do.

One of the most crucial and elemental pieces of instruction I had neglected to give my students prior to the guided imagery was the right to dissent! I did not explain to the class that if any uncomfortable emotional situations arose while they were in the process of the guided imagery, they had the absolute right to remove themselves mentally or even physically from the room. I had forgotten the most critical safeguard required in an activity with such a potentially broad emotional base. I was so ready to tackle the entire activity that I lost sight of the most significant element, the students, and their ultimate safety.

No matter how much you think something through, making sure you eliminate factors X, Y, and Z and promote factors A, B, and C, a gigantic shift occurs when you are actually in the classroom teaching. Even if the teacher cannot predict which direction the activity will take, being prepared for diverse reactions will truly be putting students' needs as top priority. This is essential when using guided imagery.

While my lesson included insights, epiphanies, and the opportunity to make connections with the students in a million different ways, I had somehow neglected to eliminate a horrible creature. This was period two on my third day at the high school. This was my initiation into the pure essence of teaching.

A Student Teacher's Response: Being Human and Caring from the Heart

This case touched me personally as well as professionally; I identified strongly with both the student and the teacher. Looking ahead to student teaching and beyond, I can clearly see the need to establish a safe environment for all students. There should be no questions in the students' minds regarding their personal security before an activity commences. I admired the fact that the student teacher admitted an error in judgment and sought to correct it. It is important to remember that we are capable of making great strides and experiencing severe setbacks. But more importantly, the student teacher brought humanity and caring to the situation.

Although he or she carefully planned the exercise, the instructor in this case failed to give the class the right to dissent during a guided-imagery activity, which thereby would have provided the students with an out if the activity troubled them. We need to understand that all students are different and that guided imagery has the potential to evoke suppressed memories. Also at issue is the presence or absence of an established safe environment for the students. These issues appear to be interrelated. If a safe environment had been created, the students would have had the opportunity to dissent during the introduction of the activity. This all goes back to the adage "Know your kids." In defense of the student teacher, however, I wonder if sufficient time for this investigation was allowed. I would guess that it wasn't. On the other hand, just how much can a student teacher learn about students, especially their personal issues, in a short period of time? Then it becomes an issue of being unprepared for the consequences. Maybe professional judgment and careful selection of words were more the issue in this case.

The case asks another important question: Just how involved should teachers get in the private lives of their students? It was a judgment call on the part of the student teacher not only to apologize to the student but also to give Iris her or his home phone number and offer further assistance. A teacher may not always take this course of action, but in this case, since the student was new to the school and was staying at a halfway house, I consider it to be not only good judgment but an act of honest caring and compassion.

A Teacher's Response: Cutting the Risk of Aerial Maneuvers

Over the years, I, too, have been amazed at the power of guided imagery as a teaching/learning strategy to stimulate students' imagination. Forming mental images and verbalizing mental processes are the mind's way of symbolically representing meaning (Paivio 1971). When my students "return" from any of their frequent guided journeys or, as I like to call them, "aerial maneuvers," I am always amazed and thrilled at the richness and individuality of their experiences and the meanings articulated from these images as we debrief the experience together.

When I consider using guided imagery, I must know what it is I do. What is the nature of guided imagery? How does it work? Almost instinctively we modify the environment to create an atmosphere that is safe, serene, and inviting. Students are asked to sit or lie comfortably, to close their eyes, music faint in the background, the lights dimmed, the teacher's voice soft and suggesting. And what happens as a result? Muscles begin to relax and breathing deepens. Brain wave activity slows from the active engagement and alertness of "Beta" to the deep relaxation of "Alpha," where students begin to access the wealth of creativity that lies just below their conscious awareness. In the Alpha state, the left brain dominates, students begin to "think" in images. The teacher must select words carefully as words have the power in this Alpha state to conjure images which trigger memory and emotion. In this case study, we see the potential negative "dark" power of one single word: "Creature."

I make it a rule to script my imaging sessions according to my lesson objectives. If I wish to open the students entirely to the wealth of their imaginations, I use what Joe Norris refers to as "divergent imaging" (Norris 1995). For example, in an exercise where I expected students to "build" their secret hideaway in mime, I prepared them with a guided imagery that enabled them to search for their own images rather than merely accept mine. In it I used a lot of questions:

> See a place, a safe and secret, magical place. Where is this place? Inside or out? How did you get there? Climb? Crawl? Fly? Walk? Swim? Is it bright or dim? Warm or cool? What are the smells? The sounds? In this special place, where do you sit, stand, lie? See yourself sitting or lying there now. Feel the textures. See yourself, safe and secret in this special place.

My goal was to have each and every image unique and special. So my words seeded for divergence of image.

However, in preparation for their story theatre presentation of the story of Hansel and Gretel, my seeding opted for "convergence." I wanted their images to maintain the essential givens of the story but diverge in the rich varieties of detail that imaging can provide.

> See the witch's gingerbread house, tucked and hidden there in the deep, dark woods, smoke curling from the sugared chimney.

Developmentally, what we now know of the brain and cognition indicates that most students until the approximate age of eighteen years may not yet be able to maturely rationalize their emotional responses to experiences. Thus, I choose never to use divergent guided imagery to stimulate dark images and emotions. I can save those exciting, dark images when working from a given text or story. The dark images then are safely framed and objectified as having happened to another person in a story time and place.

For me, the issues in this case study are not so much about permission to dissent as about lesson design. We should not feel or be rushed when doing an imaging exercise. We must know why we are choosing imaging as a strategy and to what purpose. We must consider our students' cognitive and affective development. We must choose our words with care and most particularly we must be aware of the power of this strategy and its potential to "spirit them" to places unknown where we may not keep them safe. If that happens, then we do what the student teacher in this case did so wisely, debriefing all students but giving the gift of time and concern and caring to one in particular.

Over the years I have found these steps helpful in making my guided imagery successful:

1. Establish a physical environment that allows the student to relax (lights dimmed, soft music in the background, laying or sitting with eyes closed or head down, breathing softly, experiencing the quietness of their relaxed body).

2. Coach the students to center themselves, to stay open to the experience and images that may come to mind, to feel safe and secure, to trust in guidance and in this exercise. I also suggest to them that imaging doesn't always work for everyone and that's OK. I suggest that whatever happens, they remain quiet, relax their bodies, and breathe softly.

3. "Take-off": Create a written script to seed images which will aid them in a safe and rich journey: "See a time when . . . ," "Hear the sounds of . . . ," "See on the white screen of your mind. . . ." I try to stay away from seeding words which may force a cognitive response such as "Think of a time when. . . ."

4. "Landing": As I conclude the exercise with students, I try to avoid "crash landings," rather I focus on "gentle touchdowns." For example, "I am going to count to 10. When I begin, start to stretch out, then roll to the side, and by the time I reach 10 you should be sitting up with your eyes open. Take your time. Ready . . . 1, 2, 3. . . ."

5. Debriefing: It is imperative that students have the opportunity to reflect upon and share their "maneuvers," their experiences, their

journey. As Joe Norris (1995) points out, "Good [teacher] questions need to be thought through and can be based on the aims of the lesson; e.g., 'How many of you were in a rowboat, in a canoe, in a sailboat?' Get at some of the depth that the exercise was attempting to elicit" (8).

I highly recommend guided imagery if it will aid you in meeting your teaching and learning objectives. It is a valuable tool in any classroom when we wish to problem solve, to remember and reflect, to create, to fantasize, or to prompt an emotional response to events. It needs to be treated as a special strategy that takes time and thought and planning. And sometimes, yes, it is a risk. Drama is a social art form. It's mostly about, as Dorothy Heathcote once said, "man in a mess" (Wagner 1976). As a drama teacher I will not shy from messy, risky business, as that is what fosters creativity and growth.

Extensions

1. All teachers struggle to find the balance between teacher and confidant. It is often difficult not to react immediately to the behavior of a student. What are the consequences of becoming too emotionally involved with students?
2. The cooperating teacher questions the student teacher's decision to give Iris his or her phone number. What other ways could the student teacher have made him- or herself available to Iris?
3. The student teacher is reminded to allow students the right to "dissent" or to "opt out." What are some techniques that you might use in your own classroom to allow students to discover and challenge their own comfort zones within the safety of the classroom?
4. The particular strategy discussed in this case, guided imagery, has often been criticized because it is not specifically a drama strategy and the potential exists for manipulation. Discuss the pros and cons of using guided imagery.

TRIALS AND TRIBULATIONS OF GUPPIES AND PIRANHAS

Here, the student teacher experiences difficulty when moving from a collegial to an authoritative stance with a group of grade 9 students.

Aahhhh! Student teaching! A chance to explore, test, learn, examine, and rethink many of my ideas about the wonderful world of teaching.

My placement was at a junior high school. Everything seemed to be going well; I was slowly improving and building my confidence working with the grade 8 and 9 drama classes, when suddenly an incident occurred that threw me for a loop. It was a very negative experience that will stick with me for the rest of my teaching career.

Explaining what exactly took place is a little difficult. I was working with a grade 9 class composed of eight boys and four girls, doing a unit on puppetry. Seven of the boys had been thrown out of all other elective classes; drama was the option of choice for the girls. Before I began teaching, my cooperating teacher told the students that they were to cooperate with me or he would find another activity for them to do: written work. This made me a little nervous because I thought, "What kind of management problems am I getting into here?" But the first two lessons went well even though my classroom management techniques were tested.

My university instructor came out to observe my third lesson. The students were constructing fairy tale puppets. To my amazement the students were like little guppies. They all awaited my instructions and presented very few management problems. The group went to work quickly and effectively. I felt after this class that I had a basis for building a strong working relationship with these students.

The next two lessons also went well; there was focused work while the students finished their puppets and prepared to hand them in. The sixth lesson surprised me, however. The students were to hand in puppets and then start to analyze each fairy tale in preparation for their production. We were then going to do a relaxation exercise during which the students would focus on the character of their puppet to help them with their character development and with the script analysis.

Easier said than done. It was a Friday afternoon—the weather was warm and the students had spring fever. My spirits were a little low that day, distracted by family problems and the news that a very well-liked actor had died. As the students came into class, we talked about the actor's death. Two students came in late and I asked them to wait outside. They had been regularly late and, as my cooperating teacher suggested, I had let them know that the next time it happened they would have a sixty-minute detention. The response I received was not one I expected: "You're only a student teacher and you're gone at the end of this week. We're not going to go to any stupid detention." I decided not to fight with them, so we returned to class.

I began to take attendance. Every name was greeted with a smart-mouthed comment from one or two students, forcing me to stop and focus my attention on the initiator. Eventually I began to ignore what they were saying, but it still took me ten minutes to get through the attendance of twelve students. Meanwhile another student got up, opened an outside door, and started throwing snowballs at the gym class outside. Two other students wrestled on the floor, breaking a set piece stored in the room. I used the only bit of energy I had left to get their attention and to deal with each problem that had arisen.

I thought I had refocused them, but I should not have assumed anything. We discussed evaluation procedures for their performances, and I provided my expectations. I told them that their puppets were due at the end of class; four students interrupted, saying that they did not have enough time. I was tired of fighting them, so I gave the class twenty minutes to finish.

At the end of twenty minutes, I asked them to put away the puppets and materials. Total chaos broke out. Some students took swords from the storage cupboard and started sword fighting, others threw things around, others played with their puppets behind the puppet theatre, and others resumed the wrestling match. They had turned into a bunch of piranhas. I tried to react, but all I could do was just stand there trying to figure out where that group of guppies had gone. My cooperating teacher walked in while I was trying to sort out the chaos. The students ignored me when I tried to get their attention. When the cooperating teacher tried, they also ignored him. He walked over, grabbed one of the wrestlers by the shoulder and yelled at him.

I stood there in shock. I was very hurt that my cooperating teacher had to save my skin. He told them that they were to listen to my every instruction and without a word carry them out. They then worked like the guppies I had once known. At the end of class, the students and I sat down and discussed what had happened and how we were going to improve for the next class. We shared the blame for why the class was "unproductive" and agreed to make things work for the rest of the unit.

This particular incident occurred not because the students were bad, but because my planning was not appropriate. The group I was working with was unique. For the first four classes, they were allowed to do individual work without much direction from me. The students, therefore, were not expecting me to begin leading them through exercises and asking them to follow very specific instructions. I should have prepared them for group work, which they would need to complete their puppet assignment.

Furthermore, I did not take into account how my cooperating

teacher dealt with this particular class. He later told me that about once a month he had to scrap the entire lesson and go with what they wanted to do in order to keep them focused. Usually they were prepared to work by the next class. He told me that the class was about due for one of those days, and they probably thought I would respond in the same way he did.

My own low self-motivation and energy also contributed to the problem. I knew that the group took a lot of energy and that for them to stay focused, I had to believe in everything we were doing. That Friday was one of those bad days, and my cooperating teacher reminded me that a teacher has to find the energy—it may be in a reserve bank or it may be in the students, but it must be found. If I hadn't stayed up late the night before marking exams, I would have had more energy to deal with my classes. My cooperating teacher and other teachers on staff agreed. Teachers who are really involved in extracurricular activities sometimes have problems because they do not eat well, exercise regularly, or get enough sleep.

Do all these things make a difference in the way you teach? Yes, I strongly believe they do. If I had had more energy in that particular class, I would have been able to read my group better and realize what they needed, instead of trying to go on with a lesson that was loaded for disaster. You have to deal with the days when they are piranhas, ready to eat away at your lessons.

There are two words I'd use to describe what I have learned from this teaching experience: flexibility and energy. You must be flexible, not only with your expectations but with your lessons as planned and your lessons as taught. You can have bad days, and so can your students, so always have in mind something else to do. Also, energy is contagious. If you have a high degree of energy, so will your students. If your energy is low, then your students will never buy into the lesson. By taking care of yourself personally, your energy will increase. I plan on remembering this piece of advice.

This experience was probably the best thing that could ever have happened to me. I was obliged to take the time to examine my lessons, management styles, and personal commitments. Many people say that they go into teaching to work with kids and that it is these special moments when something really clicks with one kid or a whole group that keep you there. I believe I chose teaching because I can continually learn and challenge myself. I know there will be some great days and I definitely know now that there will be some not-so-great days, but I am looking forward to each and every day that I can say, "I learned something today."

A Student Teacher's Response: Little Fry Take Big Fish

The central issues in this situation seem to be class management and lack of information, which led to inflexibility and loss of control. Had the student teacher known this class expected to be able to break the flow of the planned lessons once a month or so, she or he might have been able to assess what was going on and act accordingly.

The most urgent issue is to get the class back on track so that students are working cooperatively with and not against the student teacher. The most critical learning is what the student teacher realized upon reflection: the lesson planned for this particular class was not suitable. The student teacher allowed too much independent work at first, so that the students weren't accustomed to follow when he or she began to lead.

I think it was the responsibility of the supervising teacher to lay out, right at the beginning, what the class was like, including the students' expectations. Had the student teacher known this to begin with, instead of finding out the hard way, she or he would have had a head start in planning the unit and lessons. I think it was misleading to give the impression that the students were used to heavy discipline when, in fact, they required a more flexible approach at first.

The teacher overreacted a little to the students in the hall. The problem was that the student teacher didn't make them accountable for the rules that he or she had laid down. As a result, the students reacted negatively, creating chaos in the classroom. I think the students felt that the student teacher had become a flimsy authority figure who they couldn't respect.

I've learned how important background information is. If a teacher hints to me about management problems, I then ask for specifics. I have learned the importance of being in control, even on a low day, and following through on rules or clearly deciding on other consequences. Making sure lesson plans fit the level, interests, and capabilities of a specific group is extremely important.

A Teacher's Response: We're All in This Fishbowl Together

In any teacher-student relationship there will be good days and bad days. In making the bad days better, I think a lot depends on our expectations and the waters in which we ask our students to swim.

Despite the fact that seven of the boys in the class hadn't chosen to be there, the class was able to function fairly well. One bad day out of four is pretty darn good. The boys hadn't had success in their other electives and had been "thrown out." Drama has its own management problems, but the curriculum is open enough to accommodate diverse student interests and abilities. I can often accommodate those difficult students; even students who "don't like drama" can end up having a meaningful learning experience.

I've experienced the "guppy" phenomenon described by the student teacher; there were times, when I was being supervised, that my students really rose to the occasion. Surprisingly, even students who had given me a hard time all term were good as gold—hardly recognizable. Conscious or not, this is an opportunity for students to send a message. The message they send, I believe, is a pretty clear reflection of the teacher-student relationship. Are you allies or are you enemies? As teachers, we need to nurture a feeling of alliance. Students know when you have their best interests at heart. But that doesn't mean they're going to be "guppies" all the time. In any good relationship, individuals may take bites out of one another—a la "piranhas." This is part of the learning process. Because of the power differential between a teacher and students, I think that it is important for a teacher to allow students to provide feedback by taking a little nibble now and then.

I have swum with guppies and with piranhas. I've also experienced the all-out piranha attack described. The issue, I think, is one of communication between teacher and students. Like an iceberg, a large part of the message remains unspoken. On the day described, the students' behavior communicated a clear message. It's not that the lesson was inappropriate—earlier, successful classes showed that students' interests and abilities were being met. The students just weren't ready for relaxation exercises at that time. In a situation like this, the teacher has two choices. Abandon the plans altogether—like the cooperating teacher did from time to time—or find a way of bringing the students from where they are to where you want them.

Now, there are no guarantees in working with piranhas. They are an unpredictable species, and I certainly don't claim to have all the answers. But, this is where a drama teacher's bag of tricks comes in handy. On this day, the students seemed to be just brimming with energy they needed to burn off before they could get down to work. The teacher wasn't providing them this outlet, so they were doing it for themselves. The problem is that letting them go crazy for five or ten minutes usually ends in someone getting hurt. The teacher needs to find an activity to focus their energy; an active game like "Blob Tag" might do the trick, where those tagged become part of the ever growing blob. Following an activity like this, the teacher then wants to bring the level of energy down with a focus/concentration exercise. In drama, games and exercises serve as effective management tools. Students are having fun while doing the work.

Classroom management is about communication, about hearing what the students are trying to tell you. Warm-up games and exercises are valuable parts of a drama lesson—for getting students ready for drama, for teaching skills, for introducing themes. They are more than just games. They should be an intrinsic part of where the lesson is going.

Extensions

1. The student teacher mentions that he or she did not include any management items in his or her planning. What might such items or strategies be (examples: establishing conventions, sequencing, nipping in the bud)?
2. The student teacher who has responded to this case suggests that the management problems came about because of a "lack of information." What do you need to know about a class to help you with planning? How will you get to know that class? How will you determine what a suitable plan is?
3. The author of the response believes that learning as much as we can in advance and preparing thoroughly will solve many of our management problems. What purpose(s) does a plan serve?
4. The student teacher believes it is important to respond to students with energy, and she or he shares with the reader what she or he needs to do to keep her or his own energy levels high. Do you agree with her or his conclusion? If so, how will you do this?

MUSIC TO TAME THE SAVAGE HEART

In this case, the student teacher tries to establish a link between teacher and student while finding a comfortable spot on the continuum between teacher and friend.

On my first day at the high school, I was both nervous and filled with anticipation. Fortunately, I had on my power tie and stick deodorant, and I was determined to psyche myself into a superficial state of self-confidence. I had walked into an uncharted frontier, armed with my pedagogy and my lesson plans—only time would tell whether I would come out victorious.

I knew that I needed to mingle and mix with the students. But I was a student teacher: Should I approach the students as a "teacher" or as a "friend"? Drama involves a lot of collaborative group work, and the teacher must juggle both these roles in order to get students working with rather than for or against him. My cooperating teacher was a virtuoso; I observed in awe as she made casual conversation with students, putting them at ease and enabling them to express themselves freely while commanding their respect.

The grade 11 students were rehearsing scripts they had written based on their work with a short story. There were five groups of five students dispersed around the classroom, engrossed in their work—an excellent opportunity to walk around the room and touch base with them. It was then that I received what I can only describe as a slap in the face. I had been listening to a group that consisted of four boys and a girl. I found the disproportionate number of boys in this group somewhat odd, since the class only had a total of six boys. At the time, however, it was a minor detail. This particular group was reading through a script that had a few witty moments, but for the most part, it was just weird.

I found myself trying desperately to find the hidden thread that would somehow connect the bizarre amalgamation of ideas. I deduced that one of the boys had written, typed, and made copies of the script for the other members of the group because a lot of the language and humor seemed to float right over their heads. The script told the story of a teenager named David who has moved to a new neighborhood as a result of his dad's recent job transfer. While trying to make friends, David gets involved with a cult that wears garbage cans on their heads. The members of this cult coerce David into drinking "the brew" (blood, I assumed) as part of their initiation into the group. They then proceed to organize an armed robbery that is eventually busted by the cops. All of this and more was condensed into a script that was no more than ten minutes long.

As I listened to them rehearse, I asked what form of power they were focusing on. They paused for a moment and looked at one another. None of them, except Chris, the author of the script, seemed to know. He retorted sarcastically that it was about the power of cults. Although I sensed some hostility, I thought that I might listen a little longer before moving on to the next group. Chris suggested that somebody should tell the student teacher to get lost.

I felt that if I had moved immediately to the next group, it would have appeared as though I had let this student intimidate me. I knew that everything I did at the very beginning of my practicum would affect the way students would perceive and treat me from then on. In all truth, I was shaking in my boots; I didn't even know any of their names or anything about them, and they didn't know anything about me. Something told me that Chris and I were going to find out about each other by the end of that day.

"Was that written in the script or did you improvise that on the spot?" I asked, hoping that our conversation might take a humorous turn. He dodged the question and suggested that I wouldn't last long in this practicum. I had heard of students trying to "push the teacher's buttons" to get a reaction and Chris certainly didn't hold back.

Masking my nervousness with humor, I asked, "Why? Are you going to try and break me or something?" He snickered to his friends and reminded them that they had managed to get rid of their previous student teacher. Trying to shift the focus from me, I said, "I take it you didn't get along with her?" He claimed that she had "sucked."

I wasn't sure what to say or if I should say anything at all. I didn't want to give him the opportunity to cut me up. I stood there for a few seconds, seconds that felt like an eternity, just looking at him, searching for a sign that might give me a clue as to what he was thinking.

My power tie pressed securely against my jugular like a noose and my deodorant failed miserably. As I walked away from Chris' group, the lone girl reassured me that the others were all talk and were just testing me. Still, I was going to have one eye over my shoulder at all times, just to be careful.

As time passed I learned a lot about Chris and his friends. They were very content to be different. In fact, one might say they prided themselves on being thespians, of sorts. They never felt the need to rehearse. They would simply read through the script and then five minutes prior to performance, do a quick haphazard run-through. Invariably their performances were chaotic.

Chris, in particular, was a rather intriguing individual. He was smart, definitely above average, and he had a wide range of interests and knowledge. He was an honors student and a surprisingly good writer, which explained why he wrote all the scripts. It appeared, however, that he had gone to great lengths to conceal his intelligence. I think that Chris honestly believed that his bizarreness distinguished him from the rest of the class.

My cooperating teacher and I agreed that the only way that the four gentlemen in the group would contribute anything of benefit to the class would be to split them up. This was a delicate matter requiring great tact because my cooperating teacher had given students autonomy in choosing their groups. If it appeared that I was only splitting up Chris' group, the entire operation could blow up in my face. I explained to the entire class that, although it is fun to work with one's friends, it could be stifling to personal creativity. One of the challenges of drama is to develop strong interpersonal skills that enhance the creative process. This prepared the entire class for the new groups that I would establish.

For the collective dama, we created a fictitious community with a social hierarchy consisting of counselors, hunters, and slaves. The process built up to a ritual in which each group presented offerings to their god. However, as the drama unfolded, several dimensions of power emerged—oppression, resistance, rebellion, fear, and violence.

The group drama signaled a significant turning point in my relationship with the students, especially Chris. I could sense that he was interested, though he made tenuous efforts to conceal it. I also began to see traces of respect surfacing; the resentment and defensiveness that had startled me in that first class slowly diminished. This was partly due to my role playing as the leader of the community. However, despite the fact that a sense of community was developing, Chris and I still didn't know much about each other.

Another turning point occurred during a ten-minute break between the double block of drama. Chris and his friends routinely listened to CDs during this time. I knew many of the musical groups they played, but I never mentioned it. One day they played a CD by Faith No More and I asked them who the Faith No More fan was. The expression on their faces was one of complete disbelief. "You listen to Faith No More!?!" they yelled. In the blink of an eye I was transformed from the nerdy student teacher with the tacky tie to someone that shared a common interest—music.

In subsequent weeks my cooperating teacher and I created an assignment in which students explored the power of music in their lives. During this time, I had numerous informal conversations with students about their musical tastes, their favorite groups, songs, and videos. And it was during this period that Chris and I became friends. He would bring CDs to class and lend them to me, and occasionally I would do the same. Our conversations were not exclusively about music, though music was always an easy way to begin.

The day Chris came to me with a story he had written, I knew that he really trusted me and saw me as teacher and friend. I knew that this was a big risk on his part and I didn't want to jeopardize his trust. He didn't want me to correct mistakes or give any suggestions; he just wanted to see if I liked it. He sat by my side and watched my expression as I flipped the pages. Whenever I laughed, he asked me what part I was reading. In truth, I didn't understand a lot of the story; however, the parts that did catch my attention possessed Chris' trademark wit.

My last day was touching and a little sad. As Chris shook my hand and thanked me, I realized that one need not choose between being either a teacher or a friend; sometimes the best learning experiences are those in which this distinction becomes a little hazy. Teaching is much like friendship—it requires a constant give-and-take by both parties to keep the music alive.

A Student Teacher's Response: The Power of Persistence

Through reading this case, I have learned the value of getting to know your students on a personal level. Finding out about them and what they are interested in might help you reach your educational goals, because you can connect what they are learning with what is happening outside in the real world. Not only will this encourage students to have fun, but it may also help them realize that drama can bridge many gaps. Connecting real life with school will help them academically.

In this case, the student teacher used music to reach the students. He didn't give up; there is something to be said for persistence. One must understand that some students will learn one way, while others will learn a different way. Sometimes a teacher must stray from the lesson plan just to be real. Students can relate to adults as long as the adults are attempting to relate to them. Instead of approaching a situation as a supervisor, one might want to approach the situation as a peer. However, one must be very careful to command the same respect that she or he will need to oversee the class as a teacher.

I have learned that one must think of many things even before stepping into the classroom. Will I ever know everything? No, but I am challenging myself every day to get better and better at my art.

A Teacher's Response: Friend or Friendly?

What is the difference between being a friend of the students and
   treating students in a friendly manner?
What is the purpose of teaching drama?
Is teaching about controlling student behavior?

Looking at the last question, one finds an interesting paradox. A quiet, controlled class—every teacher's dream—would in reality be a nightmare if this were a class of teenagers. Teenagers constantly challenge the nature of the universe. Reflecting on my years in the classroom, I have come to believe that our task is to take the students from where they are and challenge them to use their strengths and skills to grow emotionally and intellectually. We must come from a teacher-to-student orientation in decision making to a student-to-teacher direction. These students are not adults with all their goals in place, and I don't believe we should treat them that way. If they don't challenge, question, and provoke, the future will be bleak. My response to the question "Is teaching about controlling student behavior?" is *"No."* A teacher's role is to demonstrate and show how cooperation and working in unison benefit us all and help us achieve our goals. A teacher observes, questions, and challenges.

In this case, the student teacher questioned his role and relationship in the classroom: "Should I approach the students as a 'teacher' or as a 'friend?'" In my experience, students don't really want a teacher to be their "friend." I can treat them in a friendly manner, but I always remember that I am there to provoke not accept, to reprimand not ignore. As a teacher I am more than a mentor; I must encourage their independence, but at the same time restrict them for the greater good of all. I must respect them as individuals yet have them consider the needs of the group as a priority; and above all, I must put the needs of the students ahead of my own. So what is the role of the drama teacher? This is a question that can only be answered by each individual.

Extensions

1. When the student teacher begins his or her practicum, the students are writing plays from short stories. What sorts of skills do drama students need to successfully complete this assignment? Plan a similar unit that you might teach during your practicum. What short stories might you use? Refer to Tarlington and Michaels (1995) for ideas on building plays.
2. The student teacher worries about the dilemma between being the student's teacher and friend, while the teacher's response counsels that the teacher is not the student's friend. Where do you place yourself on the continuum between teacher and friend? Discuss the advantages and disadvantages of each.
3. The student teacher talks about regrouping the students to break up groups of friends. What are the advantages and disadvantages of allowing students to choose their own groups versus assigning students to groups? What are some ways students can be assigned to groups?

4. The student teacher who responds notes that it can be helpful for teachers to find out what students are interested in before planning instruction. List some ways in which you can identify student interests and apply these to your own planning. If you are currently in or going to a practicum, try these out.

3

Classroom Climate:
Working with Groups

FINDING A FOCUS THROUGH PLAYBUILDING

This case describes how a student teacher went about adjusting lessons to a nontraditional school day and involving the grade 9 students in setting their own classroom rules.

When I first entered the drama room, I hoped I was prepared. I had my lesson plans that I had spent the weekend honing and shaping; I had my unit plans prepared for the entire three months. The school had recently adopted the Copernican timetable. Instead of a course taking a whole school year to complete, each course fit into one semester and students would take four courses per term. The thought of having the kids for two and one-half hours a day was a bit daunting. On the other hand, I could imagine time spent on deep insights, exciting discussions, and guided-reflection periods.

But I soon realized I wasn't prepared. I was faced with thirty-two "yakaholics" who didn't give a whit about deepening their experience. Half of them took drama because woodworking was full, or because you had to know how to draw to take art, or they considered drama to be an effortless way to get credit in something. The other half were expecting musical theatre and/or skit work.

When I asked them what they wanted from the drama course, we were constantly interrupted by people chatting to each other in complete disrespect of the speaker and by constant put-downs. I insisted on two rules: No one would speak twice until everyone had spoken once, and there were to be no put-downs. But these rules seemed difficult, if not impossible, to enforce.

Next I tried laying out a long piece of paper and felt pens across the room. I asked the students to come up a few at a time and write any words or ideas that they connected with the word *drama*. I thought this silent activity might focus them. They all came up together, even though I asked half to sit down. Most students wrote appropriate words while some students couldn't resist drawing nasty cartoons. I then asked them to walk around the paper, reading out loud the words they had written. They did a kind of party hop as they stepped all over the paper, ripping and tearing it as they giggled and laughed.

I stopped the exercise and insisted that they sit down and take a few minutes to talk about respect and listening. I tried simple listening and trust exercises next. They complained loudly that they were above all that and had done it all in grade school. I tried to explain that trust building was never something one outgrew, that professional actors had to build trust with each other. Still they complained.

We tried the "Rain Forest" exercise, in which a group creates the sound of a rain forest by working as a group. The first four times we attempted it, at least one person could not resist making a stupid remark or deliberately destroying the rhythm. I was determined we would continue starting and stopping until we made it work. The fifth time was a charm. They all remarked on how "cool" it was to make the rain forest. I got a discussion going about why it worked and how drama games and exercises need structure to make them satisfying.

I thought I had them. In the next set of games and exercises, however, we were back at square one. I had dropped all my lesson plans and was scrambling through my unit plans trying to grab them with something. The thing they finally settled on, in the last half hour, was an improvisation game called "Bus Stop." It was familiar, they felt safe, and they focused.

The next day I tried to use "Bus Stop" and improvisation exercises to explore the ideas of motivation, objectives, and blocking. Though it was somewhat successful, by and large, chaos ensued.

On the third day I told them I was feeling frustrated because of all the chatter and put-downs. I went over my two rules and asked them to come up with their own rules and their own consequences. It took a long time—most of the period in fact—and they complained wildly, but we did start to get somewhere. We wrote the rules and consequences on a long sheet of paper. One of these rules was "no put-downs." If someone put another person down, she or he had to sincerely tell the person three things she or he liked about that person. Although this was a time-consuming practice, I think it was useful. Of course, there were always the exploiters who put people down just to slow down the class.

Fortunately, some of the real dissenters transferred out of drama. But four remained, and it became a constant fight to see who would keep the class' attention, them or me. There were lots of trips to the office, but not enough stays after school, which might have been the more effective route.

Despite the fact that this group never fully learned to listen to one another, they were for the most part a highly intelligent group, and the things they did accomplish were very good indeed. How much more could they have done had they been able to listen! They began telling each other to "shut up," yet the next minute the person saying "shut up" would be one of the chatterers. The most effective classroom management strategy I found was to time them. I would look at my watch, counting the minutes wasted, and we would make up the time by staying after class. But there were buses to be caught and lessons to go to after school. Ultimately I didn't follow through with this technique. As my cooperating teacher said, I needed to be more forceful.

Although classroom management was an ongoing concern with this group, we had some magical moments together. We did Neelands' (1984) *Crookham*, a kind of mystery/witchcrafty role drama about a town in the 1600s. Students seemed to work well as reporters and townspeople, manipulating secrets and attending meetings. The few dissenters were quickly hushed by the rest of the group. Next we did *Rose Blanche*, a story by Roberto Innocenti (1990), about a young girl who helps holocaust victims. We found connections from this story to their grandparents and World War II. Cecily O'Neill's *Way West* (O'Neill and Lambert 1982), about traveling the Oregon Trail in the 1840s, had its highs and its lows. The high moments came when we were saying good-bye to a family that decided to go back, and a "hoedown" that erupted spontaneously out of a sharing of hopes and dreams. While successful, I can see now how I could have deepened these moments by drawing on the students' knowledge first.

Perhaps the most successful part of this class was the decision to do playbuilding with them. Although they started, having brainstormed first, with the idea of a modern teenage comedy, what they really ended up wanting to say was that being a teenager is difficult, confusing, and full of pressures and worries. They chose the monologues to be presented by secret ballot. These included a powerful one from a student whose mother had recently died, one about being Chinese Canadian, and another about how hurt a girl was when her mother left the family.

The playbuilding began with a tableau during which each person came on stage, took a pose, and said what being a teenager was like. I used "Theatre of the Oppressed" techniques (Boal 1979) such as "Cops in the Head" and "Voices in the Head" to explore what it is like to be their age. These exercises were then choreographed into the performance. The students set their monologues in a school and some of them used their bodies as lockers, water fountains, and a vending machine.

I tended to lose them, however, when I started getting them to explore teen problems. Although they enjoyed the library research on such topics as AIDS, teen pregnancy, teen crime, etc., the topics were too broad, too imposed by me, and too removed from them. But I was in too deep at this point to change. I needed help. I talked with my cooperating teacher, who told me to keep it simple; my methods teacher, who said to make it relate to their own lives; and a visiting professor at the university, who said to find a holding frame. I incorporated this good advice as best I could and had the students explore teen pregnancy in terms of their own lives. We eventually decided the play was about how we treat others. The holding frame was a tour through a museum of teen problems, the tableau being the main consistent element throughout.

The dress rehearsal was a chaotic nightmare, but the first performance was surprisingly good. During the second performance, some students threw balls of paper onto the stage and clapped inappropriately backstage. This upset the committed ones, and my cooperating teacher and I had to confront the class. Our lecture on trust was a bit didactic, but I think the point was well taken. Students wrote apologies to the class.

In the end it was that crazy grade 9 group that taught me about high school teaching. I learned that listening and trust building is best when it comes out of the drama itself instead of being forced on students. I learned that I need to trust my own thinking and not to be afraid to be severe sometimes. I realized that although planning must be tight, one can't be too attached to it, and I learned not to impose my ideas unless they connect to the students' lives.

A Student Teacher's Response: Expect the Expectable

As drama teachers, it is very important for us to prepare for everything. This, however, is difficult and is why it is so important to be flexible. Teachers need to have backup activities that meet the same objectives so if the first exercise bombs, they will have something else that can accomplish the original goals. If the original activity does not work, part of the problem might be that the teacher has not grabbed the students' attention. In classroom management you must start with the basics: rules, a safe environment, and students' interests. There are three things that I want to remember about classroom management.

First, it is important to inform students of my expectations. If a student does not know the rules or does not know what the teacher expects of her or him, then how would the student be able to feel safe in that classroom environment? Before the student teacher starts teaching, he or she could ask the cooperating teacher about the backgrounds and interests of the students.

Second, students need a safe environment to work in. Grade 9 students are going through many physical and emotional changes and need support and structure in order to feel safe. A student's safety comes from trust and familiarity. Trust needs to be developed over time, while familiarity can develop from structured rules and interesting topics. In this case, once the student teacher discovered the interests of the students and began to work with role dramas that students could connect to, classroom climate improved.

Third, when we put so much time and effort into planning, it is difficult to give it up, but if our lesson is not working, we need to follow our "gut instinct" and change our plans. In the beginning, the student teacher recognized the need to change direction; the teacher said that she or he scrambled through the units to find something to do. The playbuilding unit worked well because the student teacher used the students' interests and they found material that had relevancy to their lives.

When I student teach, I hope to follow the first step of Cangelosi's (1999) teaching process model—determine the needs of the students. I also want to be sure to talk with my cooperating teacher beforehand to learn more about the students, their prior knowledge, and their interests. I will also establish my expectations on the first day. As a teacher, I can only expect so much from my students. I am not saying I will have low expectations, but, if I do my work and find out about the students in the class, then I can expect the expectable.

A Teacher's Response: The Answer

Welcome to the Drama Classroom or, using a term that I prefer, the Drama Lab. It is real; it is fun; and it is *challenging* and *rewarding*.

To me, teaching drama is showing students how to tell their stories and practice the skills that they will use for the rest of their lives in work, at home, and at play. This is where the student teacher found success despite the discipline problems. However, telling our stories is risky; there can be joy and pain. To create a safe environment we develop trust—trust in action and word. We must demand respect for everyone in the room—students and adults, male and female, gifted and struggling. This is the issue the student teacher faced: the students did not respect or trust one another or themselves. To instill discipline, the teacher tried a variety of techniques: remove disobedient students, enforce rules with detentions, etc. The teacher was trying to be "more forceful."

In our society students are not always taught or shown respect. For example, some stores limit the number of teenagers allowed in at a time and the scrambling of security when a young person enters is designed to intimidate. Our school practices teach our students to be self-centered. At school we see the honor roll, the prestige of athletic competition, the refocusing of programs to individualized computer instruction and modularization, and the concentration on job skills rather than education.

By contrast, in the drama classroom we share our work in a protected, comfortable community of learners. We use the techniques of theatre as tools rather then ends. We heighten our ability to work together by exploring ideas, concepts, issues, etc. Whatever will capture the interest of the students will become a means by which our students will be able to learn, to improve communication and caring. To do this we start at a level the students are comfortable with and progress as far as time and their abilities allow.

We must realize that building community takes time; it happens in stages, and in many cases the students regress, bringing frustration to both themselves and the teacher. When this happens, students and teachers must become more flexible and open. All at once, those "wasted moments" become educationally sound. When this happens, you will have found the answer to the problem of the lack of respect. Here lies the solution.

Extensions

1. The student teacher notes that the most successful work the students accomplished was the playbuilding based on teen issues. How did their preliminary work in role drama prepare the students for this unit? How can you prepare your students for their own playbuilding unit? See Tarlington and Michaels (1995).
2. It is considered important that students take ownership for their

own learning. What other kinds of drama units might allow student ownership? What differences might there be when students work from a scripted piece?

3. The students in this case were involved in setting their own classroom rules. What strategies can the teacher use to prepare students for the negotiation necessary when developing a behavior contract?

4. Read several discussions of student rule setting in classroom management texts (e.g., Cangelosi 1999; Charles, Senter, and Barr 1999) and compare and contrast these ideas with those in drama methods (e.g., Clark, Dobson, Goode, and Neelands 1997; Morgan and Saxton 1987, 1991).

SILENCING THE KETTLE DRUMS

The student teacher in this case has two junior high classes with contrasting management problems.

Silence can be golden. For a teacher, shouts of enthusiasm can be just as golden. In the classroom these golden moments are not as easy to create and maintain as one would imagine. Often you just have to settle for silver moments, unsure of how to create that precious management of sound.

Two classes, of equal size and equal level, can be so similar and yet so different. I will begin with a brief description of the two drama classes: Jan's and Bob's. When I began teaching, I had an advantage with Jan's middle school drama class that I didn't have with Bob's. I had previously spent a week with Jan's class, team teaching an orientation/introduction unit for which I had a hand in the establishment of the class rules and expectations. Although I conferred with Jan regarding the rules we would be implementing, the time spent establishing rules with the students was valuable to me. It was the beginning of the new semester, and the class was but a single day old when my colleagues and I took over. I returned a week later to begin my practicum, teaching that class as well as others.

Our goal was to create a special bond during orientation in the first few drama classes, establishing expectations and building trust and confidence. These are the backbone of an effective classroom, regardless of subject area. Jan's class and I hit it off. Enthusiasm was high. Life was good. I did not feel discouraged about entering Bob's class even though I had not been involved with the students' orientation. Regardless of the differences between the classes, I anticipated a good experience.

Being a student teacher with a vast array of drama courses under my belt, I felt confident and eager to begin my new adventure. Besides, I was not alone. I had been placed with another student teacher, who would be team teaching the two drama classes with me. With a fresh outlook, the opportunity to team teach, a confident drama background, and two similar classes, I thought I would have no trouble. The experience did not turn out as I had expected.

Jan's class had a fairly even makeup of grade 7 to grade 9 students. The grade 9 students, as expected, were more comfortable and boisterous than their younger counterparts. Enthusiasm was high as the grade 9 students volunteered for activities, spreading the energy around to the others. Before long, however, a problem emerged. A group of five in grade 9 began talking out loud and shouting insults to other students. While we were explaining activities, they would be talking or goofing off; while others were performing, they would shoot out comments. Life was not good.

Bob's class, on the other hand, had a different problem. There was a complete lack of enthusiasm from the majority of the class. Jan's class was wonderful in the fact that there were these five students who would always jump up and exhibit quality work. When asking groups to present in Bob's class, often the response would be a simple "No." This threw me off because I didn't expect a response so simple and succinct. The intention was obvious. It was not the fact that they were not prepared or that the topic of the scene was personal; they just did not want to get up in front of the class.

In Jan's class, changes had to be made. As the saying goes, "You must silence the kettle drums so you can hear the piccolos." The few were dominating the many. We took a number of actions to diffuse this problem in Jan's class. At her suggestion, students with unacceptable behavior were temporarily removed from the class. At other times, we would address the situation head-on after low-key responses to the disruptive students had failed.

At one point, a student whom I had removed from class got into trouble in the hall and was sent to the office. Later we talked. The next day was better, but still not up to acceptable standards. It was not this one student; it was the group. I tried breaking the students up, which was useful because it spread the enthusiasm around to other students, but soon the grade 9 students began shouting across the room to one another. I did not want to lose their enthusiasm, but these five were destroying the class with their utter domination. What to do next?

In Bob's class, we tried several different things to defuse the participation problem. First, we took the class a step back from working on more involved improvisation activities in which each student would be in the "spotlight." We went back to some orientation-type games because we felt that there was still a lot of tension and a lack of trust among the students. This solved the problem for a short while, but the semester could not continue with just simple orientation games that neither challenged the students nor focused on the curriculum. I found myself trapped. For whatever reason, the class could not move on from playing games to a higher level of understanding. What to do next?

I tried to pinpoint the problem with the two classes. Were there two different problems, or would one solution be the key? Jan's class was excellent in one way: There was no problem with any of the activities because of the enthusiasm of the grade 9 students. They were always the first to volunteer, motivating the others. There was a competition between them that drove them to bigger and better things. Yet, self-discipline was a problem. On the other hand, Bob's class was very easy to manage. Because they were so quiet, there was little difficulty in getting them to settle down and ready to begin each class. While I was talking, attention was fairly good, and there was minimal student chatting, yet participation was poor. Each of the classes was locked into a mode dictated by a few students.

After talking with the two teachers, my partner and I decided on specific strategies for each class. In Jan's class, accountability seemed to be the problem. While constant informal assessment took place, we were not formally evaluating all of the activities and projects. Even being a good audience member is vital for the success of the class as a whole. Why shouldn't audience participation be evaluated? Students often asked how much an activity counted toward their grade. We hoped that including more formal evaluation would give these students the nudge they needed. Although holding students more accountable might have aided in solving the problem, I didn't expect the difficulty to be completely overcome. I also needed to sit down with each of the students on a one-on-one basis and review my expectations and their responsibilities. They would be the ones to decide their own fate.

We decided to try a different course of action in Bob's class. Bob suggested the problem might be the lack of large group work. Those who were not as inclined to get up and perform would be able to "get lost in the group" to a certain extent. At least they would still be taking part in the activities. After some large group work, the groups could begin getting smaller, putting more and more focus on the individual. Hopefully this would ease the students into the spotlight, eliminating the problem of lack of participation.

No single strategy was the key. Because there were many interlinking problems, many different solutions and strategies needed to come together to create a productive learning environment.

A Student Teacher's Response: Fine-Tuning the Kettle Drums

In "Silencing the Kettle Drums," the student teacher had difficulty dealing with the variations in classroom dynamics. Jan's class had five grade 9 students who grew to dominate and disrupt the class, while Bob's students were uninspired by what was happening in the classroom. In both classes, however, the problems seemed to stem from the teacher's focus on "performing." Perhaps the students were not ready to perform and needed more time in exploration in order to feel more comfortable with themselves and one another. The student teacher noted that the grade 9 students in Jan's class were enthusiastic; however, their enthusiasm turned into unfocused energy as the term progressed.

Jan's boisterous grade 9 students were testing the limits of the student teacher. The student teacher felt that she or he had a "special bond" with these students after having spent a week with them before taking over. However, it seems that the students needed to be reminded of the class rules or at least be made aware that the same rules existed even though their regular teacher was not present. Those rules had to be enforced.

When these boisterous students started shouting insults across the room, the teacher might have stopped the activity and reminded them of the classroom rules. If insulting a classmate was not addressed in any of the rules, then that would have been the perfect opportunity to include it in the list of unacceptable behaviors. If these boisterous students persisted, the teacher could have spoken to them in private to see what the problem was. After hearing the problem from the students' point of view, a plan of action or a contract could have been worked out on a more individual basis.

A way to stop the grade 9 students from "goofing off" while other students were performing would be to not do performance-type activities. The teacher could have chosen activities that engaged the students in their own drama, so that they did not have to become audience members for someone else's drama. If, for some reason, the teacher insisted on doing performance drama, then he or she should have been very clear as to the duties of an audience member. Again, the classroom rules must be enforced.

The teacher might have mistaken nervous energy for enthusiasm. Because unfocused energy is usually disruptive, the students needed more focus. Giving a nervous student the spotlight could encourage her or him to goof off as a cover-up. More trust exercises might have given the members of the class the confidence and self-esteem they needed to push their drama further.

Bob's students, on the other hand, needed something to motivate them. I think the root of the problem for this class was the same as it was for Jan's. Because these students were obviously too self-conscious to get up in front of their peers, performance was not advisable for this group. The student teacher could have started at the level they were at. If they did not want to get out of their seats, then the teacher could have facilitated a radio drama. Then students could have found a topic that interested them, possibly motivating them to explore the issue further. After that, the teacher might have been able to get them up to "do" the drama that they had created in their minds.

The student teacher claimed that he or she had to revert back to orientation games. Redoing an exercise is not a reversion—if that is where the students are, then that is what the students need. The teacher might have fostered more critical thought by asking questions about the nature of the games and the strategies used to play them. The purpose of playing games in drama goes much deeper than just having fun.

In conclusion, both classes seemed to be intimidated by the performance aspect of drama. The teacher could have silenced the kettle drums by taking the emphasis off performance and putting it on self-exploration. In order to reach the unenthusiastic students, the teacher could have provided them with a problem to solve or the students could have chosen their own. Once the topic or theme had been established, the teacher could have begun the drama at the students' level. If games are all they can handle, then play games—but let them discover the learning in those games, and eventually they will want to push themselves a step further.

A Teacher's Response: Finding Answers to Classroom Management Issues

It is true that the "music of the classroom" is not always mellow and sweet to the ear. Kettle drums will boom and even the piccolos will screech out from time to time. The objective of effective classroom management is to create an environment of harmony in the drama class.

Part of this task is to spend a significant time at the start of the year or semester working with students on developing a trust-filled and safe class environment in which everyone feels comfortable participating in both the spotlight and a whole-class project. However, just because the class has participated in a good two weeks or so of sharing, trust exercises, and the collective building of expectations for classroom behavior, it does not guarantee that one or more of the students will not take an opportunity to challenge these rules later in the year.

In a perfect world, I often imagine that the ideal drama class would be filled with starry-eyed students gazing up at their teacher with rapt attention, the room vibrating with their energy and concentration as they involve themselves completely in learning through the drama . . . and then I laugh. In a perfect world, maybe, but in a real drama classroom, the focus is not always so complete or powerful, if, on some days, the focus is there at all.

In some drama classes, there are usually a few students who are not prepared to participate appropriately in classroom activities. Perhaps they are tired, hyper, excited, sick, angry, depressed, or just trying to be "cool." Maybe it is early in the morning, just before or just after lunch, or the last class of the day on a sunny Friday. As teachers, our responsibility is to find the right combinations of management strategies to pull those boisterous attention-getters and those disinterested nonstarters back into the lesson and participating at a level that is comfortable for everyone. And no, it is never easy. However, it is important to act swiftly and firmly, always ready to listen to students in a dialogue or a group discussion about those same behavior expectations everyone agreed to adhere to in the beginning.

In the case of a classroom heckler, the one-on-one conferencing is certainly effective, reminding individual students of their responsibility to respect their classmates so that drama can happen. In the case of the passive nonparticipants, altering lesson plans so that ensemble or group drama is emphasized over the individual "spotlight" performances helps to draw out the shy or insecure students.

There are times when it is necessary to stop a lesson and remind the whole class about the importance of trust and mutual respect in the drama class and lead them in one of those great trust activities from earlier in the year. Ask the right questions, listen to the responses, and help the class refocus its attention on appropriate classroom behaviors. Then the kettle drums, piccolos, and strings will play in harmony.

Extensions

1. The students in Bob's class seemed reluctant to perform individually; the student teacher response suggests that more student-generated drama could be an answer. Assume that you are getting ready to teach a class like Bob's with many inexperienced and reluctant students. List some of the activities you might begin with to build trust in the class and enable students to share their work comfortably.
2. Refer to texts in educational psychology and adolescent development and find information that might explain why students might be afraid of a performance class. Plan activities that specifically address your research.
3. The student teacher decided to make the grade 9 students in Jan's class more accountable by grading audience participation. What criteria would you use if you were taking this approach? Working with a partner, make a list of other measures you might take to increase student accountability.

4

Classroom Climate: Working with Individuals

QUITE A QUIET STUDENT

This student teacher describes the steps taken to give an extremely shy junior high student enough support to eventually prosper in a drama class.

I had difficulty sleeping the night before as I anxiously awaited the first day of student teaching. I envisioned myself at the front of the classroom with thirty students looking at me with eager eyes. I thought of the teachers who had influenced me as a student. I dreamed that I would somehow touch the life of at least one student during the semester and help that student become a stronger individual. I thought about how I would treat each student with respect and encourage my students to work toward their individual and ultimate potential, no matter what their level of interest in drama.

Because the school had adopted a middle school exploratory learning program, elective classes, including drama, were one-semester courses. Student teaching in the second semester was just like starting in September because I had all new, inexperienced students. I also had many students who did not choose to be in drama but were placed there because it fit into their schedule.

During the first week, we played a couple of simple theatre games that introduced the students to drama without putting them "on the spot." The games allowed me to start learning the students' names and interests. Already, I felt a connection beginning with some students that I did not feel with others.

I always expected the interest level of my students to run the gamut from overly enthusiastic to extremely shy; however, I never expected Amy. Amy was a quiet student who sat at the back of the room, virtually unseen and unnoticed by everyone. In fact, I didn't notice her until the second week.

I wanted all of my students to participate at their comfort level; however, Amy did not want to participate at all. I tried the bold approach by simply inviting Amy to join, but she declined. At the time, I was not aware of Amy's degree of discomfort. Most students joined in the games, but there were a few in each class who were reluctant, not unusual with junior high students. I reminded all the students that part of their grade depended on participation. Later in the week, I previewed the first couple of assignments to make them aware of what I expected. I thought that by allowing Amy some time to process the assignments, she might get ready to participate.

Unbeknownst to me, Amy was downright scared to be in the drama class. During the second week of school, Amy arrived late to class and I allowed her to watch the rest of the lesson. I knew she had been at the counselor's office. At the end of the class, Amy quietly told me she did not want to do any acting in front of the class because she felt intimidated. She had trouble telling me that she was afraid to be in the class. She was so distraught that earlier she had cried in the counselor's office. She requested a schedule change, but the counselor suggested she try the class for a few more days.

I felt a sense of loss for Amy and myself. It seemed as if I had failed a student only two weeks into the school semester. I wanted to help her be a part of the class, but at the same time I did not want to overwhelm her with so much support that she would not want to try at all.

My cooperating teacher and I agreed that Amy needed drama, as it is an ideal environment for all students to be able to find themselves. Drama allows students the freedom to express themselves in a safe and nurturing environment. Amy needed the encouragement of her peers to help her gain a sense of individuality and personal strength through a feeling of community.

I told Amy that the first assignment was with a group and the following two assignments were nonverbal, movement performances with a partner. I hoped that having another person on stage with her would make her feel more at ease. I suggested that she give drama a few more tries before she decided to leave. With some reservations, she agreed to stay.

The first assignment was "Who, What, Where," in which students randomly select a line from a pile of cards and create a scene. They determined who they were, what they were doing, and where they were. Students could choose up to five people to participate in the scene. I asked students to volunteer to perform and if they were called upon to present because they had not volunteered, they would lose points.

Amy did not volunteer during the first two days of performance, nor did she give any verbal feedback on the performances she had seen. She merely sat at her desk and watched. I knew she was nervous and I was concerned about giving her enough space for her to feel her way into the class on her own. I knew, however, that sooner or later she would have to participate. I talked with her after the second day of class about the assignment.

Again, she told me that she was afraid to speak in front of the class. I suggested that she choose several students she had seen perform to help lead the scene. I hoped that she would at least have the chance to be on stage and possibly begin to see how much the students were enjoying themselves.

Amy chose five strong people from the class to perform with her. Together, they determined that they were friends, at home, deciding what they wanted to do on a Saturday afternoon. The other students suggested activities to Amy during the scene, while Amy said her line. She completed the scene successfully and even got caught up in the action, improvising a couple of lines. I felt a small spark of joy; she had participated even more than I had expected. I hoped that this effort was a trend that I could continue to foster.

During the next several weeks of school, the class moved into a paired mirror exercise. Amy partnered with another relatively shy girl in the class, Robin. The class was given one day to rehearse. During the rehearsal time, I allowed them to use a private rehearsal room. I also gave them some encouragement and pointers. When it came time to perform, Amy did not wait until the end to volunteer. She successfully performed with Robin. I let out a slow sigh. I considered this simple act of volunteering another huge step for Amy.

One month into class, I felt that Amy's comfort level and participation had increased significantly. She showed tremendous improvement in her actions and skills, even as quiet as she was. Nevertheless, her mother requested that Amy be moved from drama into a study skills class because of low grades in her core courses. My heart sank; Amy had made so much progress.

When Amy approached me about her mother's request, she told me that she wanted to stay in the class. She said that she really liked the class and did not want to leave. I was elated. Luckily for Amy and me, the study skills classes were full. Encouraged, I let her know that if she ever needed to do homework or study for a test, so long as her work for drama was completed, she could use one of the rehearsal rooms. She agreed and thanked me.

Amy's progress continued slowly but I had to make concessions. I permitted her to do one spoken presentation alone after school. I thought about my decision long after I had given her a high grade on her performance. Was I encouraging her or holding her back? The answer came when the class moved on to the next unit.

Amy and Robin chose to perform their next project in class together. I anxiously watched them rehearse, encouraging their creative input into the scene and hoping that they would volunteer to perform during the first two days. Amy told me that she had been talking with her mother about the class. She let me know that she was working on a dialect for the scene, if that were acceptable. Encouraged by her peaked enthusiasm, I agreed with a triumphant "Yes!" Amy and Robin performed this scene on the second day with few difficult moments. The scene was better than I had ever anticipated, and Amy even signed up for the school musical!

Looking back on the semester, I know that my accommodations and understanding supported Amy. Amy, of course, greatly influenced her own progress. She became an active member of the class and her self-confidence grew. I learned that even the quiet students need my attention.

A Student Teacher's Response: It's All About "Withitness"

In this case, the student teacher took the time and energy to make Amy's success a personal goal. The first step in the process for the student teacher was to gain Amy's trust and provide her with as many safety nets as possible. Providing a personal rehearsal space, agreeing to an after-school presentation in the absence of her classmates, and continual positive feedback demonstrate the nurturing environment that the student teacher created for Amy. In the absence of this special learning environment, it is likely that Amy would have very quickly removed herself from the class.

This case is a good example of the right way to do it. It is in recognizing and understanding the special needs of students like Amy that a good teacher becomes a mentor. It is this individual treatment, or what Nachmanovitch (1990) calls "presence," the ability to extend yourself, to go beyond just seeing what's happening to responding to what you're seeing that brought a successful conclusion to this situation. My cooperating teacher calls this "withitness." This necessitates making time for one-on-one communication with every student in the class, formally or informally. What matters is that the teacher makes personal contact with each student, providing opportunities to make the class the best experience for all.

To have a presence in the classroom goes further than one-on-one meetings. It means taking what we learn from these meetings and applying it to our classroom, using the information our students provide to empower ourselves as teachers. As the student teacher in this case learned, Amy's fear was rooted more in having to speak on stage than in just being there. Understanding this, the student teacher pushed her to go on stage but made special allowances regarding vocal performances. In doing so, the teacher was leading Amy toward improvement at an appropriate pace. The student teacher assessed Amy's individual needs and then sculpted her learning environment to best meet these needs. This handling of the situation perfectly illustrates my cooperating teacher's concept of "withiness."

Making special allowances for students may create other issues that must be dealt with. From my point of view, a teacher needs to make allowances for individual differences. The risk is that this special treatment might be interpreted by other students, teachers, or even parents, as favoritism, and hence might foster feelings of resentment and jealousy. Nevertheless, it must be done in order to provide a suitable learning environment for all students—our number one job.

After becoming aware of our students' learning needs and then providing them with the tools and structures to meet these needs, the last step in the equation of "withiness" is assessing progress and providing feedback. In Amy's case, the student teacher carefully monitored her progress and provided Amy with constant reinforcement. If students are ever going to fly, we must be willing to carry them until they are ready.

The important thing for teachers to remember is that students will progress at their own rate, not ours, and we cannot get discouraged if the process seems to be taking longer than we would like. For some students, six years of drama might not yield the results that this student teacher was able to see in Amy in only one short term. We must be proud of and cherish any progress that occurs. That is where the satisfaction of teaching comes from—knowing that we made a difference.

A Teacher's Response: It's Never Too Late!

This case should be required reading for all administrators from K to 12. It demonstrates, without a doubt, the uniqueness of drama—a field of study that not only promotes learning in the traditional way but fosters emotional growth as well.

This case demonstrates what teaching is all about. The student teacher response helps us focus on the main points of classroom practice:

- listening
- individualizing instruction
- maintaining flexibility in presentation of assignments

I believe the most important aspect is that of listening. In the drama program, without this skill, there would be nothing else. What special means of instruction could you devise if you have not found out what is causing the problem or even realized that there is a problem? You treat fear much differently than lack of skill or just plain obstinance.

One must keep in mind that solutions do not happen immediately. Over a period of time, through careful nurturing from the student teacher, Amy started to open up to try new things. Although she was still scared, the fear was no longer controlling her.

The uniqueness of drama—the safety, the support, and the fostering environment provided by the student teacher—allowed Amy to find success and her own empowerment.

Extensions

1. What is the difference between a drama class that emphasizes student performance and one that suggests students present or share their work? How does our choice of terminology and approach convey certain student expectations? With these approaches, what implications can there be for both very shy students and extroverted students?

2. There are many students who are chronically shy in classrooms. Requiring them to perform in front of the class or even to answer questions out loud may be asking more than they can handle. Design a series of orientation activities specifically for the very shy student. Remember as you do to also consider how you will assess class participation.

3. Hot seat one to three volunteers in role as a student like Amy. What can you learn from this student's perspective that you can apply to your own planning?

4. How would you label yourself? Shy? Extroverted? Laid-back? Energetic? How might an extremely shy student view you? Consider how you might have to modify your interpersonal style to be most effective with an extremely shy student.

THE IMPOSSIBLE, UNBEARABLE STUDENT

The student teacher in the following case learns to see a high school student with a lot of personal problems as an individual.

Before I began student teaching, I asked myself what were some of the things that I would never do as a teacher. I came up with quite a list, but at the top of my list was my biggest pet peeve: I despised the way that some teachers did not understand that students come into the classroom with various backgrounds and experiences. I vowed that I would not fall into this trap. Unfortunately, I learned the hard way that if you do not continually guard against trivializing your students' lives, you might become what you do not want to be. This happened to me with one of my students, Craig.

My student teaching placement was at a high school where I had the opportunity to teach two beginning, one intermediate, and one advanced drama class. Craig was in two of the classes I was teaching as well as in the advanced drama class my cooperating teacher was still teaching. In intermediate drama, we had begun blocking a children's show consisting of four fairy tales that we would be taking to various elementary schools. Craig had two parts in the play, parts he had expressed enormous interest in during auditions.

Craig was a talented young man, very outgoing and boisterous; nevertheless, I found him to be quite overbearing, insolent, and sometimes downright impossible to work with. Although he had many friends and was never without a girlfriend, most of his peers did not like to work with him.

Craig had a dark side. He disliked taking direction and sometimes added inappropriate dialogue and/or movement for the sole purpose of getting a laugh. There were times when he angrily refused any suggestion made to him. It appeared to me that he took everything said as a personal attack. He had also been sick before I met him and was frequently absent, making it difficult to rely on him for anything. It seemed his personal life was adversely affecting the way he behaved in class, but I did not understand the extent of these problems; I thought he was just being difficult.

A number of times at the beginning of the semester, Craig and I butted heads. During rehearsals he told me that I was stifling his creativity. Instead of working, he began to close down and so did I. I began to dread having to work with him and enjoyed the days he was absent. I discussed the situation with my cooperating teacher, and I learned that, although Craig's attitude had indeed changed somewhat over the school year, this behavior was normal for him. Craig had moved out of his parents' home and was living in an apartment with a friend. He was trying to support himself by working part time and he was not succeeding.

One afternoon everything came to a head. Craig had been particularly difficult that entire week. He was still ill and was not getting any better; he was completely exhausted and irritable and seemed to be taking his anger out on everyone. By sixth period on Wednesday of that week, his mood had gone entirely black. In the past I had tried to talk to him, but by now I was so frustrated with him that I did not want to bother. I felt that he was just trying to get sympathy. Although I knew that as a teacher I should not back away from him, I did not know what to do. I was not sure that the stress I felt working with him was worth it. Thinking back to my education classes, I remembered being told that you could not save them all. I was not sure I could or would be able to do anything to help Craig. Even now as I look back, I do not have a clear answer as to how to handle a dilemma like this.

Craig was supposed to be in the auditorium rehearsing with his group when he burst into the little theatre and began storming about. When I asked him what was wrong, he flew off the handle and spouted a stream of obscenities about the people he was working with. Normally I did not tolerate this kind of behavior, but he ran out of the room before I had a chance to react.

After school, while my cooperating teacher was at a meeting and I was in the office working on the computer, Craig walked in. He closed the doors and asked if he could talk to me. I dreaded what he was going to say. Suddenly this boy who had been overbearing and attention-seeking began to sob. He was not surviving on his own; he needed to work, but he couldn't because of the rehearsal schedule. He was not eating properly because he could not afford food. He was sick and not getting any rest because of the crazy schedule.

Then the real heart of his troubles began to surface. He had been moved from place to place so many times that he was barely in grade 11 at the age of eighteen. He had no hopes of graduating before he was twenty. He wanted to get into a program for students over age eighteen but couldn't because he didn't have a car. He could not go home because his parents were encouraging him to be independent. When we discussed the situation further, I learned that his parents were still supporting him and helping him in many ways. Overall, the problems facing him were much greater than I could have imagined. He was not trying to be a troublemaker, but every behavioral problem came from what he carried daily into the classroom. Although this did not excuse everything, I began to understand him better. He wanted to drop out of the show but felt that he would let the others down. I reassured him that although we would miss him, we understood and would not think any less of him.

As a result of our discussion, we devised a way for him to stay in school and in drama. He looked much more rested and his health improved. More importantly for me was how our relationship improved. I validated his situation and helped him work things through.

Craig has made me reevaluate the way I looked at my students. He reminded me that I need to see each student as an individual and to know what is going on in his or her life before I make judgments. In educational psychology, we discussed how often a student's behavior is a reflection of what is happening at home. Remembering this information may have prevented me from feeling the amount of stress that I felt when dealing with Craig. It is very easy to fall into the position of being an all-knowing, and often uncaring, teacher. To prevent this, I believe all teachers must remember how they wanted to be treated when they were students. They must balance this with their positions as teachers.

I am thankful that everything worked out as well as it did. Although Craig remained boisterous and outgoing, most of his behavioral problems diminished. All I had to do was understand and validate his problems—from there we could work out a solution.

A Student Teacher's Response:
Enthusiasm, Humor, and Dedication

I believe that all teachers, from elementary to postsecondary, can learn from the experience of this student teacher. We must make an effort to listen to our students, to be compassionate, and to try to help solve problems in a positive manner. I can achieve this through conversations on a casual basis with my students on topics that interest them. Inviting students into my office, listening to their concerns, and having outside agency numbers and addresses available if they are needed are other ways I can achieve these goals. If a student is disruptive or unfocused, I can pull her or him aside when class is over and ask what's wrong.

Understanding and validating students' problems is an area in which many educators lack sensitivity. Although this case ended with a reasonable solution, what would have happened if the student had not spoken to the teacher on his own? Often educators accuse students of being extrinsically motivated, only concerned about their marks. However, the same accusation can be leveled at teachers. Teachers are often so busy trying to manage classrooms that they focus on the external behaviors of students rather than recognizing the internal motivations behind these behaviors. Thus, we begin to ignore the problem students or we deal with problems by hoping they will go away.

The student teacher was falling into this trap. Rather than trying to help the student, the student teacher was thankful when the student wasn't around. It is rather ironic that the student, out of an intrinsic desire to improve his own behavior, taught the student teacher a lesson about looking for internal motivations. The student actually became the teacher and the teacher the student. This resulted in the student teacher listening to the student, validating the concerns of the student, and then taking steps to help relieve the situation.

As a future teacher, the most important step I can take is to remain passionate, demonstrating my love of teaching to the students through enthusiasm, humor, and dedication.

A Teacher's Response: Breaking Through

We've all met students just like Craig and have been left with the same nagging questions: "What can I do with this student? What can I do to make a difference in how this student is working and behaving? How can I continue to teach this class when this student is being so disruptive?"

Craig presented a particular challenge to this novice teacher, yet I suspect that he may have done so with even more experienced teachers as well. The teacher began to pigeonhole Craig in the "difficult student" category and felt frustrated that he or she was "falling into the trap" he or she accused others of falling into—"trivializing" the student's life. In trying to cope with Craig, the teacher demonstrated some successful management strategies that still left him or her "dread[ing] having to work with Craig and enjoy[ing] the days he was absent."

In wrestling with what to do with these problem students who emerge every now and then, we realize that these students are exhibiting behaviors that are the symptoms of deep-rooted problems. It's ironic that the novice teacher in the study felt that others don't understand that every student comes into our classroom carrying "baggage," and then the teacher forgot her or his own admonition. However, with Craig, the student teacher was fortunate enough that a "defining moment" occurred, allowing for a breakthrough.

Ideally, an opportunity for an impossible, unbearable student to open up will occur and the student's problems can be addressed. However, in much of our teaching, overcrowded classrooms and demanding schedules preclude the ability to spend the time needed to develop the rapport to "crack open" the problem. In drama classes, however, we are more fortunate because of the interactive, personal nature of the program. However, even this does not guarantee that the Craigs of the world will not fall through the cracks and get lost in the system.

In some cases it is important to allow for some flexibility in how one balances "material to be covered" with "individualized strategy." The teacher in this case did make some allowances and give Craig some breathing room. The teacher demonstrated the ability to adapt—a trait required when trying to successfully deal with difficult students. The day of Craig's crisis could have ended less favorably. Sometimes we do get lucky. The negotiations that followed were important stepping-stones toward bridging the chasm that had for so long separated student and teacher. So many times we have to find the "magic" that will turn things around.

Extensions

1. The student teacher in this case notes that she or he began to dread working with Craig. While stress can take many physical forms, there is also a cognitive element involved. Think of a current situation in your own life in which you dread having to deal with a chronic problem. Make a list of all elements of that event that you find stressful and then a corresponding solution or coping strategy for each.
2. Student and teacher behaviors are frequently motivated by factors outside the classroom. Refer to Morgan and Saxton's (1987) discussion of "personal luggage" and consider what some of these factors could be and how they might affect students positively or negatively.
3. The writers all note that it was fortunate that the student in the case eventually came to the student teacher for help. Brainstorm some things that the student teacher might have done to help Craig.
4. Working in two groups, have one group write on a large piece of paper all the things that might have been going through Craig's mind while the other group writes down what the student teacher might have been thinking. Compare your lists and discuss what you have written. Where is the common ground? Where are there differences and to what might these differences be attributed? What have you learned from this exercise that you can apply to your practicum?

THE TAMING OF THE SHREW STUDENT

In this case, the student teacher negotiates behavior in a junior high drama class for one problem student.

I was looking forward to student teaching. My years of training at the university would finally be put to use. My practicum was at a junior high school with approximately 450 students. I felt positive and confident as a teacher; I was well-prepared and equipped with my lesson plans. But little did I realize that I would encounter a student, Karen, who reminded me of Kate in Shakespeare's *The Taming of the Shrew*, and who would push and test me to my limit.

During the first week of my practicum, my cooperating teacher was trying to complete a unit on radio plays with her grade 7 and 8 drama classes. I assisted the students with any problems. The majority of the students worked well in their groups; however, the odd student sometimes wandered around the class and disrupted other groups. When I noticed this, I would politely ask him or her to return to his or her group. Usually the student would without making any comments. But there was one individual who challenged my request: Karen. Every time I turned my back, she would sneak over to another group and begin to chat with her friends. I confronted her a second time and told her that if she strayed one more time, she would be removed from class. Within five minutes, I found her chatting with another group. When I asked her to leave the class, she told me that she could tell that we were not going to get along together. She stomped out and sat in the hall. At the end of the class, when I went to talk to her, she was already gone. Karen was absent from our next class, so I wasn't able to talk to her and would have to wait until the following week.

In the second week I was excited and ready to teach. My cooperating teacher was absent, so I had a substitute teacher with me. When my first grade 7 class arrived, I told them Mrs. Smith was absent and that I'd be teaching the class. I totally forgot to talk to Karen.

I started the class by telling the students we would do a floor-concentration warm-up. I asked them to spread out and lie on the floor. There were a few moans and groans, but everyone proceeded to do it. I dimmed the lights and asked everyone to close his or her eyes and to stop talking. When I started to work on a breathing exercise, some people began to make peculiar breathing sounds. Within seconds several people began to laugh; Karen complained loudly that this was stupid. I ignored her and asked everyone to be quiet.

After a few minutes everyone stopped talking, but Karen questioned the need for this "dumb" exercise. At this point, I took the time to explain to the class why we were doing the warm-up and how it helped them relax and prepare for the following drama activities. Karen informed me that they never did this with Mrs. Smith. At this point, I remembered what my methods professor said about giving students permission to dissent. I was not going to get anywhere with Karen, and I told her if she wished, she did not have to participate. She immediately stood up and angrily sat on the sidelines. After the warm-up, I invited Karen to join us in the next activity, which she did, and she worked well throughout the remainder of the class.

At the end of the day, the substitute teacher felt that I had done well. He recommended that I establish classroom rules and get to know the students' names as soon as possible. The following day, I took one step back and began the drama class by discussing classroom rules. Karen had difficulties with them at first, but after further discussion, she agreed with them. My next step was a name game. I was not sure how well they would react since they already knew each other's names. I told them it would help me get to know everyone and it would serve as a concentration and memory game for them. As I explained the rules, they all listened except for Karen, who leaned back in her chair, crossed her arms, and rolled her eyes.

The game required everyone to memorize each person's name along with her or his favorite food beginning with the same letter. Karen was the eighth participant of the eighteen students involved. At first it appeared as though she was getting involved in the game, but by the time we got through half of the class, she, and others, were beginning to look bored. I told the students at this point that after we got through everyone, I would randomly select individuals to repeat everyone's name and favorite food. This seemed to spark their interest. After a couple of people listed the whole group, I once again realized the class was getting restless. Karen began to gossip with her friends and I started to lose everyone's attention.

I then remembered what my methods professor stated in class about "raising the stakes" to spark the students' interest. I challenged the students to see how fast they could go around the circle. I timed each student, and the top time was the time to beat. I could not believe the change of atmosphere. It was like night and day. All of the students including Karen suddenly wanted to have a turn to see how fast they could do it. Some students wanted to try it over and over again. The class finished on a high note and the name game was a success.

In the following class, I started a unit on theatre sports. My cooperating teacher felt this would be a fun change of pace. It was Friday;

the whole class seemed to be hyperactive and it took me several minutes to get everyone's attention. I could not believe how disrespectful they were. After everyone finally calmed down, I reminded the students that when I began class everyone should listen. All but Karen appeared to agree.

For the class warm-up, I allowed three students to lead the group in a center stretch. Karen was one of them. The warm-up went over quite well and Karen appeared to appreciate being one of the leaders. Next, I introduced a couple of theatre sports games. The class was working well except for Karen and a couple of her friends. I asked them to stop talking; her friends did, but Karen continued. I gave her one more warning, but she persisted, so I asked her to sit at the side and wait for me after class. She left before I was able to speak to her.

By the third week I was prepared for Karen. I decided I would talk to her before class started. I took her outside the classroom and told her I was not against her or picking on her. I was treating everyone equally and would remove whoever was disrupting the class after I had given a warning. At this point she told me to lay off. I replied that I would if she would start to listen and pay attention in class. She agreed, but I knew she would not automatically stop talking. I pursued the matter by giving her more responsibility. I asked her what she wanted me to say in class if she started to talk again. She responded by saying, "Karen, stop it." I asked her what to do if she still kept talking and she suggested that I send her to the office. We agreed to this procedure.

Class began and our group activity was running smoothly, but I knew it was too good to be true. Karen soon lost her concentration and began to talk. I proceeded to say, "Karen . . ." and before I could say the next two words, she said, "Stop it." She totally caught me off guard by saying it herself. Karen stayed on track for the remainder of the class. For the first time I felt Karen was starting to work with me and not against me.

That week I also started to teach dance and physical education. I had Karen's grade 7 class and felt quite confident that she would behave, but I was wrong. Throughout the class, Karen and a few other girls talked continuously. I gave them a few warnings that they ignored. I finally split them up and had them sit in separate corners. At the end of the class, I spoke to each girl. When I asked Karen about our agreement, she stated that the agreement was for drama class, not physical education class. Her answer did not surprise me. We ended up agreeing that the same rules applied there.

During the last week and a half, Karen and I slowly began to understand one another. I still had to remind her a few times about our agreement, but at least she did not contest it. I felt I had partially tamed the student. I learned from Karen that I should have spoken to her immediately after an issue arose. Instead, I allowed the problem to slide, thinking that with time it would vanish, but instead it escalated. If I had confronted Karen on the first day, I would have set a better example for us both earlier in the practicum.

A Student Teacher's Response: Wouldn't It Be Great If Students Came with Instruction Manuals?

Out of all the students, Karen, the "shrew," was the most troublesome, perhaps because she did not fully understand what behavior was expected in the classroom. If Karen felt confused about the rules of the classroom or the purpose of an exercise, there is a good possibility that others were just as confused as she was but were less vocal.

Karen didn't know the rules, so she tested the student teacher's authority. Those other students who really enjoyed drama class were no doubt frustrated with Karen's behavior and resented the student teacher's attention being diverted so often in Karen's direction. Students are smart; when they see an opportunity to take some time to goof off, they take it. This situation certainly afforded them such an opportunity.

I think learning to teach is like learning how to drive a stick shift. At first, there are so many things to think about and do, all at the same time. For instance, if you press too lightly on the gas and lift the clutch up too quickly, you stall. If you do not let the clutch out enough while pressing the gas to the floor, you rev the engine really loudly, and you go nowhere. The same thing happens in student teaching.

You have what you thought was the best lesson plan in the universe, and you jump feet first into it with your students, but you go too fast, lose your students, and the lesson flops. Then you try easing into an average lesson plan, but you give too much—or not enough—emphasis to the wrong part of the lesson, your students get confused, and you cannot continue. In time and with practice, you can drive your car down the street, avoid collisions with curbs and other vehicles, shift gears smoothly, and change the radio station all at the same time. In time and with practice, I think teaching will become second nature.

Sharing experiences and challenges certainly helps the learning process. After reading this case, I have learned how essential it is to establish my expectations for student behavior in my classroom. It might make the transition for the students easier if I adopt the classroom rules of my cooperating teacher and get students to agree to extend those rules to all the classes I teach. I have also been reminded to introduce the purpose and value of all exercises, games, warm-ups, and assignments before launching into them.

A Teacher's Response: The Taming of Whom?: Control vs. Collaboration

The Taming of the Shrew is one of my favorite Shakespearean works. It is about wit and shrewdness, man and woman, and power and control. But it is the antithesis of good drama teaching. In this case we see a student teacher grappling with these very issues. Karen has become the shrew who is trying to vie for control of her destiny in the drama classroom. The student teacher quickly falls into her trap and sets up a power struggle in which no one can win. From the very first encounter, the student teacher puts him- or herself in a position of power by "challenging" and "confronting" Karen. Karen certainly had it right when she told the teacher that they were not going to get along together. The next several weeks proved just that. Many new teachers find themselves in situations similar to this. In fact, as I think back on my first few years of teaching, I can remember being in this situation many times. Fortunately, I have figured out how to avoid these confrontations.

I have been very fortunate to work with Jonothan Neelands for the last several summers. Jonothan is a master teacher who guides students through the mysteries of teaching by showing, through his lessons, the keys to good drama teaching. He believes that drama is about community building. "It is about empowerment," Jonothan says, "a difficult word." I have learned from him that the first task in any drama class is to establish an environment that makes the students feel safe, so that they can learn to trust one another and the teacher. Then they can take risks in order to learn about themselves, others, and the world they live in. Jonothan calls it "negotiating the ground rules of interpersonal behavior."

I have found that when given the responsibility for their own actions, students respond amazingly well. The student teacher in this case set her- or himself up as the power broker in the class before the pupils even knew the rules. She or he made no attempt to establish a community before she or he started to embark on the skills she or he wanted them to learn. How many of us can operate in that environment? Even as adults, we need to know what the ground rules are and what the climate will be like before we set out to accomplish anything. The teacher might have made it easier on her- or himself and the students if she or he had planned the lesson with this in mind.

The first thing any teacher must do is get to know the students in the class so that he or she knows their needs. There are many ways of doing this. One of my favorites is to ask the students to introduce themselves and tell us one good thing about themselves. Not only does this help you learn their names, but it also gives you an insight into their personalities. It reinforces the notion that you care about them and want to know about them. This would have been an excellent way for the teacher to start the class.

I have found that younger students need to know class guidelines so they know how to behave. The easiest way to set guidelines to have the students discuss how they want their class to run. Even very young children know what behaviors need to be exercised in a drama classroom. By giving them the responsibility for making the rules, you empower them to be in charge of their own actions. They will monitor their own behavior and that of their peers. Once everyone has had a say and agrees to the important guidelines, they can create a poster to hang in the classroom to remind them of their decisions. They have had an important part in creating their enivonment.

Some teachers find it difficult to let students set their own rules because they see it as losing their power in the classroom; however, teaching is not about power and control. It is about learning! Learning cannot take place unless the teacher creates an environment in which students feel safe to take risks and challenge themselves. When students design the rules for their classroom, that environment is created. When you discuss the reasons for these rules, they understand that you are not trying to be an ogre but have their best interests at heart. Jonothan says it is "what every drama must start with: an explicit structure with rules, a contract which makes it more likely that everyone will participate. Together you work out what you need as a teacher and what the students need. An impersonal set of rules for the community may have to be written down and even individually signed. If you break them you are breaking the community rules."

Community building is essential in every drama classroom. Before one can begin the rigors of the art, one must be comfortable in the environment. Students quickly sense this and must be shown that this is a place they want to be and one that is safe for them to explore who they are. Where else in our school system do they get this opportunity?

Extensions

1. In this case, the student teacher tells the story of Karen from her or his point of view. Retell the story from Karen's point of view. How might the two see events differently? What can you learn about your teaching from looking at this student's point of view?

2. The case author refers to Karen as a "shrew" student who must be tamed. What gender and power implications are raised when a student is characterized in this way?

3. The teacher's response suggests several ideas for creating a contract with students and getting to know them. What other "Getting to Know You" or personal information–sharing activities do you know that might be appropriate when you begin your student teaching?

5

Drama in the
School Community

WELCOME BACK MRS. C.—
DEALING WITH "SWEAT HOGS"*

This case discusses the problems in planning and motivating students in a junior high drama class when students who can't get into other classes are placed in drama.

When drama becomes a dumping ground for students with limited choices of elective subjects; when restricted budgets mean larger and larger classes; and when its non-core status and the general school culture create a perception that drama is something anyone can do, no amount of lesson planning can assist one in avoiding problems. This was the situation in which I found myself for two of the classes I taught at my junior high placement—two sections of rowdy grade 9 students. This issue is one that faces anyone teaching the fine arts in a public school system in these days of cost cutting and science and technology promotion. As drama teachers we must be advocates for our program, or the realities of present-day classrooms will undermine all our good teaching.

I began to wonder about this issue right at the beginning of my placement when my cooperating teacher, Ms. D., briefed me on the skills and personalities of her two grade 9 classes. She admitted they were not the best groups she'd ever had. She described them as apathetic and undisciplined. With her approval, I planned a basic improvisation unit incorporating some activities I had used with success in other situations. Ms. D. assisted me with the first lesson I taught to one grade 9 class. I was concerned with the students' inability to carry

*The term "Sweat Hogs" comes from an American television comedy, *Welcome Back Kotter.* In the show, Mr. Kotter returns to his old high school to teach a group of poor learners, potential high school dropouts, and juvenile delinquents—the Sweat Hogs.

out simple theatre games. They were very rambunctious, even with two teachers in the room. I've seen children in grade 1 better able to focus than some of these students were. I also noted that the activities just whizzed by, as the depth of involvement was minimal.

For the other grade 9 class, I modified my lesson plan somewhat to include a few more attention-grabbing activities such as "Koomallalli Visca"—an African echoing song—and a soundscape activity. I incorporated much more structure into the second class' lesson. This group was also very lively, yet the lesson went somewhat more smoothly. The group loved the soundscape activity, so I thought I was off to a better start with this group than the first.

However, as the week went on, I found that I was modifying my plans for both groups considerably. I was including many more orientation-type games and activities. I began to wonder why so many students in these classes quite obviously didn't give a hoot about drama. I had expected more from this group, especially at this point in the school year. Indeed, I was finding the two Drama 7 classes (who had just started drama in January), and the four Drama 8 classes I was also teaching, better able to handle the same material. I was curious as to why this situation had arisen with the grade 9 students in this school. Was it just a bad group of kids, or were there other factors contributing to the formation of the two classes I lovingly named the "Sweat Hogs"?

Ms. D. was embarrassed and exasperated with her grade 9 students and wanted to remove eight or nine of the troublemakers. She reasoned that this would make the class size better and relieve me of the stress of dealing with these rowdy students. In addition, it would allow the more eager students to benefit from the course. She also felt a few weeks of boring book work in the library might give the troublemakers a better appreciation of the activities in the drama classroom. While I could see her logic, I felt that this strategy would not benefit me in the long run. I needed to learn how to deal with the reality of classrooms. I wanted to give the Sweat Hogs another chance, so we decided to have a class meeting to clarify expectations and consequences.

Ms. D. and I led the discussion together. A quick hands-up survey revealed only a third of the class—10 students—had chosen drama as an elective. The remaining two-thirds—20 students—had been placed in drama either because their first choice had been canceled or because there was a limited choice in their timetable. These students got drama by default.

This information confirmed the need to rethink my curriculum. I would have to include even more orientation activities, since the majority of students in each class had never taken drama before. Also, I felt I needed to lower my expectations about the product I might hope to see. At this point I would have been happy just to get participation in the process. We might make progress together but the steps taken would be small. Also, I needed to make sure I had lots of *pizzazz* to catch and keep the attention of these reluctant participants, my Sweat Hogs.

In the next class we did upright stick tossing, a concentration and physical theatre skill game. This is a challenging and engaging activity that the classes took to with considerable enthusiasm. I also started giving worksheets to assist them in planning small-group improvisations. With the students working quietly for a few minutes, I was able to maintain better control over the general atmosphere in the class and to check in with small groups for more individualized teaching. Things slowly began to happen, albeit on a much simpler and more structured level than I had initially planned.

Don't get me wrong, there were still concerns over behavior. I had to give a few students "the boot" on a number of occasions. Often the material presented during the improvisations was poorly developed or offensive in nature. Certainly the Sweat Hogs were testing all the limits. However, I feel I made some small measure of progress with these classes. In fact, there were even a few times when the work blew me away with its wit and sensitivity.

Still, I wondered about the whole scenario. Drama's elective status means that it doesn't carry much weight in terms of whether a student passes or not. How can we gain respect for our discipline when many students view it as a time to flake off or zone out? What about the few students in my classes who had taken drama before or those who were really excited about finally having a chance to try it out? How do we keep students like these interested when progress is slowed down to accommodate the stragglers? What about the shyer ones who were intimidated by the big and boisterous boys who so often, and despite my best efforts, dominated the class? Is this fair? I think not! What can we do to avoid such situations? These are the critical questions to be asked if teaching drama is to be more than just baby-sitting the Sweat Hogs for a few hours a week.

Not long after our meeting with the Sweat Hogs, my cooperating teacher and I attended a planning meeting for all teachers of elective courses. She raised her concerns about the limited number of choices open to the grade 9 students and described how drama had become a dumping ground. One teacher responded that drama is really just a physical course anyway, so what's the difference between drama and physical education? You can be certain that we promptly corrected his misconception!

Drama must have a highly visible presence within the school. While I'm not advocating for major full-scale theatre productions, I do feel it's important to make sure that there is some type of performance or presentation of students' work. This high visibility can ensure that administrators and other staff realize just how much work has gone on within the classroom.

Additionally, I feel that drama teachers need to be assertive with administrators, making their needs known. Dumping students with varying skills and interest in a subject is problematic at the best of times. My cooperating teacher proposed an advanced class for those who had taken drama in grade 8. This might avoid some of the problems we had encountered.

Drama teachers have enough challenges to meet under ideal conditions. The drama class is a freely structured environment that many students find difficult to adjust to. Drama depends so much on group interaction and cooperation that a single detractor can bring down an entire lesson. I quickly discovered that classroom management in a drama classroom is highly complex. However, it can also be a wonderful course to teach. I certainly had moments of wonder and enjoyment with the Sweat Hogs. Nonetheless, I have learned that I will need all my advocacy skills honed and sharpened to ensure that I get what I need to be able to teach and that my students get what they need in order to learn. Even in times of restraint, compromise and cooperation can be achieved.

A Student Teacher's Response: Antiperspirant in the Classroom

I believe that the central issue in this case involves attitude and perception. The problem is not limited to the students involved. Although their behavior is perhaps the most urgent issue discussed, the critical problem is the attitude of the school toward the drama program. This was exemplified by the comment made in the faculty meeting comparing drama to physical education. This misconception of drama must contribute to the apathy of the students enrolled in the drama program. If the other teachers consider drama unimportant, then how can one expect the students to take it seriously? The fact is that in order to have students treat a course as an important component of their learning, it is necessary for teachers to acknowledge its value. The suggestion made by the student teacher that drama needs a higher profile within the school is quite correct. This may enable other teachers to appreciate the amount of effort involved in a drama class.

The students' lack of interest and focus is probably due, in part, to their limited choice of elective subjects. I agree with the student teacher: more elective choice is crucial. The fact that many of them did not want to take drama contributed to their lack of interest in the subject. However, if the school acknowledges the importance of drama as a subject, the students' respect for the course might increase correspondingly.

I think that it would probably have benefited this student teacher if he or she had created a student inventory and assigned it the first day of class. This would have given the teacher an idea of the students' interest level and potential. A student inventory would also provide information about previous experience in drama. Depending upon the kind of questions included, it would help the student teacher determine why these students enrolled. This would have allowed her or him to create lesson plans that were geared to the ability level of the students, instead of having to scrap plans aimed at a more experienced group.

The creation of a mutual list of expectations between students and teacher would have been beneficial. A list of expected behaviors might have neutralized some of the discipline problems before they had actually occurred. These agreements function as a method of creating a safe class environment in which mutual respect is established between teacher and student.

The problems of class size and limited choice of electives work against this student teacher. More importantly, these same problems work against the students' ability to learn effectively or to get individual time with the teacher. Unfortunately, the reality of the situation is such that, without an increase in government funding, teachers will be forced to work with large class sizes and these structural problems will keep occurring. I know I would not feel as confident in teaching a demanding class of twenty as I would teaching a motivated class of thirty.

A Teacher's Response: Welcome to Reality

This case describes the problems that arise because of common misconceptions that many students, parents, teachers, and administrators have about drama and the fine arts. The myth that drama is an easy subject contributes to the problem by attracting students looking for the easy A or students who need a place to go when their first-choice elective has been filled. It is possible that drama has a reputation of being easy because many drama teachers at the junior high level have to change the course content—dumb it down—to accommodate the various levels of readiness and ability amongst their students. Indeed, many students with no drama experience are placed in a grade 9 program that is supposed to be more advanced than the grade 7 program. Thus, the reputation of drama being a class that consists of skits and games is very often quite accurate.

Unfortunately, teachers of drama are not always dealt a fair hand when it comes to timetabling, student selection, and class size. The political and financial constraints on public education play a large role in the limited elective courses available at the junior high level. There are many other issues addressed here that are also out of the control of the student teacher, the cooperating teacher, and in many cases the school administrators. In spite of this, drama teachers must persevere and find concrete solutions.

The student teacher mentions that when faced with the politics associated with elective courses "no amount of lesson planning can assist one in avoiding problems." Sometimes it may seem that teachers beat themselves up planning the perfect lesson only to have it fail miserably in practice. However, my experience has taught me that a well-planned lesson coupled with rapport with students is the best way to deal with issues concerning classroom management and student motivation.

Students need to understand that drama is more than just games and that the class activities actually help develop the skills outlined in the curriculum. Therefore, it is helpful if they know this right from the beginning. Emphasis on journal writing throughout the course can often set the tone. The cooperating teacher in this case felt that "boring" book work might be a suitable punishment. I would suggest that *meaningful* book work be an integral part of every drama class.

The student teacher expresses frustration that the few keen students lose interest because their progress is slowed down by "the stragglers." A possible solution to the problem would be to raise the expectations and to change the structure of the class. If students are challenged constantly and always held accountable, the behavior and attitude of the boisterous "Sweat Hogs" might change over time.

Students need to be debriefed on orientation activities, since they won't always see the connection between certain activities and their development as dramatists. Students also need to reflect on their class work and group experiences. Planning that includes time for quiet journal writing or note taking could send a strong message to students who take drama for the wrong reasons. Additionally, administrators are likely to be impressed with the reflective times and may be more supportive of the arts.

Finally, it may be helpful if students do not see performance as an end. A "Sweat Hog class" containing boisterous boys may not be the venue for placing emphasis on performance. Students need to feel safe on stage and in front of an audience. Perhaps activities involving small-group exploratory improvisation—with the boisterous students strategically placed in separate groups or all in the same group—would allow the other students a chance to participate.

The issues discussed in the case and in this response are not going to be resolved easily. The fact that the student teacher is willing to enter the fray and fight for the fine arts shows that he or she is well aware of the politics involved in being teachers of public education. Welcome back Mrs. C. Welcome to reality.

Extensions

1. What responsibility can the drama teacher take to ensure support staff (e.g., school counselors), administrators, and other teachers understand the drama curriculum and can facilitate advisement and placement of students?
2. Because drama is seen as a social art form, it often becomes a class for students who don't fit in the traditional classroom context. When does drama cease to be about an art form and become social work?
3. The case and the responses make the point that the teacher needs to know something about the students in the class and their reasons for taking drama. What strategies can you use to gather this information prior to teaching?

THE TIME IS OUT OF JOINT: PLAY PRODUCTION IN THE SECONDARY SCHOOL

This student teacher encounters administrative challenges in directing a play.

January was the glowing honeymoon phase of my student teaching in a private school that I very much admired. It seemed to be a student teacher's dream come true. I had been asked to direct a children's play with the advanced drama class. This sounded like a real opportunity to put to the test everything I had learned. Auditions went extremely well and at the beginning of February my expectations were high and my creative juices were flowing. I was chomping at the bit, ready to go.

February came quickly and I realized that I only had twenty-eight days to get the show up. I soon found out that the school calendar for that month was filled with three-day weekends and short days because of school assemblies. There were also days off for teachers meetings and holidays. My already-shortened month was getting shorter.

Since I had known ahead of time that I would be doing a popular children's play, I had done my research early and had my directing plans down on paper. I then found out the real value of preplanning and preparation. Because I was working with the advanced drama class, I assumed the students had had more training than they had. I had only worked with this class in a limited capacity and I was unfamiliar with the students and what they knew about drama. It quickly became evident that the advanced class was made up of almost all grade 10 students with only a one-semester drama class behind them. This added a burden to my already-cramped schedule because I had to take extra time to teach them acting basics and the concepts of play production.

I knew that almost all high schools had some extra rehearsal time after the last period of the day, so I asked my cooperating teacher for time to work with the cast after school. However, my cooperating teacher told me that the school policy was that all rehearsals had to be done during class time. Needless to say, I was very disappointed. Football, band, and extracurricular clubs all had scheduled time after school, and I felt the drama students needed the same consideration. In fact, the students themselves felt the need for extra rehearsals to make up for our shortened rehearsal schedule. All of us felt the crunch.

I decided to ask the assistant principal for permission to hold after-school rehearsals, knowing that she had been a drama major in college and might understand this necessity. She said that it was proper for drama to rehearse after school and advised me to give the students a schedule so they would know, in advance, exactly which days we would use. I discussed the matter with my cooperating teacher and he agreed to a few after-school rehearsals. I did not get as many as I needed, but I was satisfied with the compromise. I was back in the director's chair.

With the extra time and commitment from the students, things started picking up. The class got behind me and worked extremely hard. I think the students felt the same crunch and were relieved to have the extra time. Everyone in the cast had a good attitude. They wanted to learn more stagecraft and came in on their own to work on sets and props.

Managing time was my biggest obstacle. I carefully planned each rehearsal. Every night I would go over my notes on the work we had just done and assess our progress. The list of things left to do seemed to grow instead of shrink. I felt that the students were concerned with only certain production elements, such as their costumes, but I tried to be extremely positive about all aspects of production. I must give them credit. They really wanted to learn and to give a good performance.

On the inside I was having a lot of doubts about the production. I felt it was technically a difficult play to mount in a school with a limited budget. I had been used to working with very little, but I felt it may have been a bad play choice considering the lack of available resources.

The confines of the school calendar and the inexperience of the students frustrated me more than anything else. On certain days I felt that behaving in a professional manner was a bit of a stretch but that setting an example was more important.

We lost a major cast member the day before the play opened, but the students took it in stride when they realized we could work together as a team to figure out how to solve the problem. The production went on as scheduled and we had some good moments to remember.

Now that it is over and done, I look back and wonder what I could have done differently and will do differently when I have my own drama program. My biggest regret is that there just wasn't enough time to fix the weak parts of the play. I was disappointed that I couldn't get more accomplished.

After talking to the students when the show was over, I felt quite differently. They told me how much they had learned and that it had been a wonderful experience. They had been challenged and had grown from the experience. However, I'm sure I learned more than they did.

Teaching drama is so much more than producing a flawless production. It is equally important to be a positive role model. I've learned that the students like to work hard if they feel they are learning and accomplishing something and this work builds self-esteem. This attitude and approach turned a less-than-perfect working condition into a positive, valuable experience for the students and student teacher alike.

A Student Teacher's Response: Taking Time to Oil the Joints

In directing a play with a group of advanced drama students, this student teacher learned several valuable lessons. The main issue, stated several times in the case, is typified by the statement "managing time was my biggest obstacle." The student teacher had four weeks to mount a production while attempting to provide a meaningful learning experience for the students involved.

The research and directing preparation were well worth the time taken to ensure that the rehearsals flowed as smoothly as possible. It's also important to know the abilities of your students and to choose suitable material. The key is to find the middle ground between underestimation and overestimation; the play must be workable and interesting, yet challenging. The play chosen sounds as though it fit the bill. The students had to work hard and cooperatively in order to create the final product.

I do not see much of a problem in seeking the approval of the assistant principal for after-school practices. The student teacher had the support of the students and was simply requesting a slight bending of the rules.

The production was successful because the students had good attitudes and the student teacher remained professional and positive. The only suggestion I could make is that ample time be provided for mounting a production. It is also a good idea to prepare a rehearsal schedule at the beginning, ensuring that the students understand when they are needed and the commitment that is expected of them. These components are the oil that ensure all the joints are working properly. The process that unfolds is a learning experience like few others. The students have been challenged to work together to create something for their own enjoyment and the enjoyment of others.

A Teacher's Response: Let's Assume

This case is a reminder to all that a play in the secondary school is not a professional production; it is a learning experience.

We also need to become aware of our assumptions and how they can cause us havoc:

1. Don't assume the class name indicates experience. Like any book, look at the actual story, not just the title.
2. Don't assume the students have experience. In many cases they are placed for timetable concerns, not for educational ones.
3. Don't assume that the school calendar will be open for your needs and not filled with other events.

When we realize that teaching requires that we get to know our students first, many of these problems will disappear or become minor irritants. When we can encourage students to move beyond where they are, learning happens.

We must also realize that there are several dos that we should practice as teachers:

1. Do check out school policies on extra- or cocurricular work. In some cases there is very minimal support for this type of activity; with some administrators, it is expected that a play will be produced, but no time is allowed for it.
2. Do meet with the administration to gain firsthand knowledge of the policies and rules that govern you and your students.
3. Do realize that a play that is produced for public performance is still a learning situation for the students. You can ask for appropriate "professional behavior," but be prepared for many lapses and be forgiving. Remember this is a growth experience.

The rationale for doing a play was summed up very nicely in the case; the students felt "challenged and had grown from the experience." If this teacher can provide these opportunities on a yearly basis, the goal of teaching drama will be accomplished.

Extensions

1. There are many aspects to a school drama program; for example, drama can be seen as an elective subject only, as a mandated part of the curriculum, or as an after-school club. Drama can also reach a wider community audience through the production of scripted dramas and musicals and student-generated plays. What do each of these approaches have to offer students? How can each contribute to the other?
2. If you know the students you will be working with in your practicum, make a list of possible scripts that you might be able to direct with them. If you do not know your group, make a list of scripts that might work with middle school students, with inexperienced high school students, with experienced high school students. Be able to defend your choices.
3. How would you develop a student contract (Neelands 1984) for a play production unit? What considerations would you have for assessing student work and promoting student accountability?
4. The student teacher in this case was concerned because he or she had

limited time to rehearse the play. Make a list of strategies you could use that would enable you to use rehearsal time more productively.

SOME VERY "SPECIAL" LEARNERS

Here, the student teacher describes the integration of four students with special needs into a middle school drama class.

Jon entered the classroom on the first day of class with high hopes. He rushed up to me and declared that he wanted to be an actor and expected to be on stage. I simply nodded my head and told him to sit in his assigned seat. Jon, who has Down's syndrome, was one of four students with special needs in my class.

The drama program at the middle school where I was placed included six forty-five-minute beginning drama classes of approximately twenty-five students each. The semester-long class was considered an elective offered to both grade 7 and grade 8 students.

Most of the students come to drama with very little experience. The students are taught basic drama skills before embarking on a production at the end of the semester. The class typically begins with group-building and teamwork activities, followed by pantomime, voice, movement, sensory awareness, theatre terminology, history, makeup, and a scene study unit during which they memorize and produce a pagelong scene with a partner. Lastly, the whole class votes on the final project. The students are given three choices: scene study, commercials, or a class play.

In the sixth-period class, four students were considered to have major cognitive disabilities, two had been diagnosed as emotionally disabled, four had a history of behavior problems, and five were enrolled in the gifted and talented program. The diverse population proved to be a challenge because accommodations had to be made for all of these exceptional students.

The four students who required the greatest accommodation were those with major cognitive disabilities (MCD). They could not read or write. Fortunately, with the help of my cooperating teacher and the special education assistant, I was able to tailor most of the activities to meet their needs.

One student, Ed, seemed to daydream quite a bit. He could speak, but when on stage, he simply froze and forgot what he was supposed to do. Ed loved the country singer Garth Brooks and could be motivated to take part in activities at the mere mention of his name. He also had a habit of making "farting" noises with his mouth, a behavior that sent him out of the room many times.

Jill had a severe speech impediment. She struggled with intense headaches that prevented her from participating most of the time. She would either come to class with a huge smile on her face, talking a mile a minute, or arrive sullen. Because she tended to tear things up, she had to keep her hands occupied. I acquired a balloon filled with flour from the special education teacher so that she could keep her hands busy.

Tina had more writing ability than the other special education students, but she was very shy. She refused to take part in activities that required her to be in front of an audience. She also had the habit of being a "tattletale." At first, I unconsciously reinforced her behavior by stopping what I was doing to listen to her. After I heard the special education aide, Ms. E., remind Tina that she was tattling again, I adopted Ms. E's attitude and Tina stopped telling me about other students' misbehaviors.

Jon understood what the concept of acting meant and would usually take part enthusiastically. Most of the time, Jon entered the classroom and happily announced that he had arrived. At other times, depending on his mood, he, too, could be very sullen and argumentative.

On the first day of class, we began with a "Getting to Know You" activity. All of the MCD students were able to take part after certain accommodations had been made. The activity consisted of interviewing a partner in order to find out five bits of information to be memorized and presented to the class on the stage. The students were given a form to fill out. Because the MCD students could not read or write, they had to be assisted by Ms. E., another student, and me. They were able to remember the facts but needed to be cued with questions when they got on stage to complete the introductions.

Jon worked with a "regular" student, Emma. Emma understood what he said and enjoyed interacting with him. When it came time for Jon to introduce Emma, he appeared to be comfortable and was able to remember some of the facts without being cued. Ed, on the other hand, stood uncomfortably on the stage for a few seconds and then began to make faces, causing laughter. At this point I jumped in and helped him finish the assignment.

Tina refused to do the assignment at all because she was having a bad day. I explained that she could do the assignment the following day, but since she was a member of the class, she would have to complete the assignment. Tina protested. I felt a little stumped as to what to do. Instead of arguing with her, I simply did not respond to her protest, but I sympathized with her difficult day. The following day, I asked Tina if she was ready and she protested. Ms. E. jumped in and took her aside. After five minutes of discussion, it was announced that she agreed to do the assignment. I later asked Ms. E. what strategy she used, and she said that she had threatened to call Tina's mother.

The four MCD students progressed slowly, but steadily, throughout the first portion of the semester. I had hoped to meet their parents during the parent-teacher conferences, but I was only able to sit down with Ed's parents. We discussed Ed's Individualized Educational Plan (IEP) and ways in which drama had helped him and could continue to help him interact with other students.

Meeting with Ed and his parents proved to be invaluable in helping me accommodate and motivate him both academically and socially. I also got helpful information about his behavior at home. For example, it wasn't only in my class where the farting noises occurred; he made these noises at home and in other classes as well. His parents and I agreed that if he made the noises again, I should call them and they would discipline him. They explained to Ed that if they got a phone call from me, he wouldn't be able to go to Jon's house after school.

It is important that the parents and the teacher of students with special needs have a good relationship. If I had met them before classes had started, I would have been more successful with Ed. In the future, I plan to contact my students' parents and the special education teacher in order to discuss the student's IEP beforehand. In a university class, I learned that this procedure is supposed to happen with every special education student. At this school, however, there was minimal communication between the special education program and the mainstreamed elective classes such as drama.

Unfortunately, other factors prevented these four students from making much progress after the first quarter. The other twenty-one students simply did not enjoy being around them. For example, Tina really wanted to interact with the others, but when she approached them, they would run away and make sounds of disgust. Because I was often dealing with other students with severe behavioral problems, I rarely had time to talk to individuals about their avoidance of the students with special needs.

At one point, however, I was able to talk to one of my learning disabled students, Ryan. He had been calling the MCD students "retards" and "idiots." I warned Ryan to refrain from this behavior or I would contact his parents. Despite my warnings, Ryan continued, forcing me to phone his parents. While Ryan's father agreed to ask him to stop making the comments in class, he said he did not believe that the "retarded kids" should be allowed in his son's classroom. He was against the whole idea of mainstreaming and felt that those particular students did not help his son succeed. This attitude shocked me, especially since his son had been diagnosed with a learning disability! The conversation ended with me stating that if Ryan continued to make these remarks I would have to send him to the office, as he was disrupting the learning process for other students. I told Ryan that regardless of his beliefs, he did not have the freedom to put down the other students. This logic seemed to work and he did his best to refrain from making negative comments.

The students in this class never did become comfortable working together. Looking back, I think it was because we did not spend enough time on "Getting to Know You" activities that could have helped the students become more comfortable with the diversity of our class. As it was, very few of the students were ready to work in groups and perform in front of others. I am reminded of Maslow's hierarchy of needs (1970), which I learned about in my education classes. In order for a student to use higher-order thinking skills, the student must first have certain needs met. Students must feel physically and emotionally safe in the classroom environment. Because I didn't take enough time at the beginning of the class to make sure that the students felt comfortable working with all the members of the classroom, my students felt emotionally vulnerable and could not express their creativity without the fear of criticism of peers.

By the end of the semester, the students with major cognitive disabilities would only work with each other; the other students worked in their own peer groups, refusing to work with others. The different cliques bad-mouthed and antagonized the others in the classroom. Even Tina, Jill, Jon, and Ed began to antagonize. As a result, the class decided to work on commercials rather than on a play, so they could work individually. Nevertheless, I did succeed in making the environment safe enough for the students to complete the commercials.

I hope to take away with me the experience of dealing with special education students in my mainstreamed classroom. The mistakes I made at the beginning of the semester might be avoided in the future if I ensure that each class successfully creates a positive cooperative learning environment. In the future, I will have devised better ways to evaluate my students' progress with regard to effective student behavior objectives.

A Student Teacher's Response: Building Community

This student teacher did what he or she could to make the classroom a positive, safe learning environment, but this was not entirely possible. It seemed as if there was just not enough trust or fellowship built among all the students for them to be able to realistically handle the social and emotional responsibility of working in groups. The teacher was unable to find time to talk to his or her class about the students with special needs; if he or she had done so at the beginning, he or she might have been able to foster trust.

Since the other students were being disrespectful to the MCD students, the teacher might have chosen to go over the classroom rules at the beginning and concentrate more on affective goals for his or her students. Neither the students nor the student teacher had the necessary techniques to help them deal with the diversity of their classroom. The student teacher didn't know the nature of the classroom; the students didn't have a good enough understanding of one another; it created tension.

In the future, when I have students with special needs in my class, I will prepare by learning as much as I can about them prior to the beginning of classes. Again, the old adage rings true: Know your kids! If I have a good idea of the composition of the class at the beginning, I might be better able to handle the things that crop up during the semester. I also realize how important it is to instill respect and create affective behavior goals for my students. With this foundation in place, I can attempt to build trust in a diverse student body and move toward working together successfully. I also have to keep in mind that students can't be rushed into working cooperatively; the classroom climate, as I've seen in this case, has to be just right. Then, I can use the information that I gather to build a positive classroom climate for all.

A Teacher's Response: Can't We All Just Get Along?

While reading this case, I remembered a quote from Rodney King. As Los Angeles burned during the April '92 riots, Mr. King lamented, "Can't we all just get along?" Since then, countless comedians, popular movies, and TV programs have all made fun of what appears to be a simple and worthwhile concept; it's simple and yet so hard to achieve. The middle school students where I work have picked up this noncomplex, even naive phrase and ridiculed it.

We seem to get along best with just a select few. Like electricity through a series of wires, we human beings follow the path of least resistance when it comes to finding people with whom we feel secure. It seems to me that we are attracted to people who are like us. With a class of highly diverse students, the teacher must recognize which students feel most comfortable with one another. From here, the teacher can reach the ultimate goal, the top of Maslow's hierarchy of needs: self-actualization, the realization of all that a person is capable of being. Truly an admirable goal and one worth achieving.

In my fifteen years of teaching, I have rarely experienced students getting along with each and every single person in the room. Now, I do not mean to imply that this was the goal, nor do I think the over-all goal—to have the class work together—is unachievable. I do think that, because of the dynamics of a classroom, like it or not, the teacher may never achieve a productive harmony. At times, the best I could achieve was to have groups of compatible students go to neutral corners and stay there, for the sake of sanity—mine and theirs. I felt that the student teacher was wise to provide several choices for final projects in which the success of each student did not depend on total group harmony.

The student teacher learned that there are factors affecting every drama class that are beyond the control of the teacher. One factor is parental attitudes, in this case, toward "special people." I wonder how many other parents in that community felt the same way. This attitude is surely echoed by the children in this class. The student teacher is correct in concluding that she or he needed to do more "Getting to Know You" activities, but in this setting, I'm not entirely sure that this would have been enough.

The time of the class is another factor that was beyond control. Seasoned teachers recognize that classes at the end of the day, especially the last class of the day, are harder to teach. Focus wanders off, for both students and teachers alike, to what they are planning to do when they get out of the classroom. In my teaching, I find that I sometimes have to have a cool-down session at the beginning of my last-period class before I can have students work with one another.

In order to succeed, I feel you need to achieve two goals. First, do the best you can with what, or in this case who, you have. Second, challenge yourself to do better the next time. It seems that the student teacher did this and has the makings of a good teacher. He or she should not be so discouraged by this particular experience.

Extensions

1. The student teacher in this case found she or he had to make accommodations for the students with special needs. Choose a unit you have planned and add adaptations and/or modifications for students with cognitive, visual, auditory, and physical disabilities. You may find it helpful to refer to a special education text or

to drama books that specifically address students with special needs, e.g. *Drama Education and Special Needs* (Kempe 1996), *Making Drama Special* (Peter 1995), and *Drama for All* (Peter 1994).

2. Create an improvisation in which drama teachers plan to include students with special needs in their classes. Consider how inclusion benefits all students.

3. Report on a company that specializes in drama with and/or for people with special needs. Some suggestions include the National Theatre for the Deaf, Pegasus Players in New Zealand, etc.

6

Expect the Unexpected

IF I HAD A DECENT ASSAULT RIFLE: BOUNDARIES IN THE CLASSROOM

During a collective drama activity, a male student with emotional problems, which he often takes out on females, disrupts his group in the following case.

I was placed in a Catholic high school. I had certain preconceptions about students in a religious setting, but I soon realized that kids are kids are kids. My case, though, revolves around one student who really made me think about teaching and my role in the classroom. Here is the story:

My cooperating teacher asked me if I would be interested in teaching collective drama to grade 12 drama students. I was hesitant but agreed to try. I planned the unit and started with a stream of consciousness writing session that allowed students to pick the theme they wanted to work with. There was one boy in the class, Rick, who when asked to write on what aspect of society he did not like, wrote that if he were to go on a killing spree he would kill police officers. This, he said, would be the perfect crime. It would prevent his arrest directly if he took out all of the police in the city. He went on to write that he also did not like women and that he would kill them too; and the best thing of all would be to kill women cops. I read this over wondering what exactly I had wandered into. My cooperating teacher said that Rick's response did not surprise her because he had had years of counseling, multiple suicide attempts, and family problems. This did not reassure me.

I decided to have the students read their work in small groups in order to pick out themes from their writing. I chose the groups for this project and I specifically placed Rick in a predominantly female group, making him accountable to his female peers for his comments. The students, however, knowing Rick better than I, were only mildly disturbed by what he wrote and dismissed it. I think that they did not know how to handle Rick either. They understood how precarious his emotions were, so they chose to let things go.

Rick's group had some trouble coming to consensus on a theme, so the members took a vote and chose "government conspiracy." The cooperating teacher felt that this topic would require too much research and advised me to give the group a choice between this topic and one chosen by another group. Rick thought that the other theme was "cheesy and stupid" and railroaded the group. Someone within the group suggested that they do something on death and the afterlife, and after a short discussion, they agreed. Rick complained the whole time, issuing ultimatums about what he wanted and did not want to do.

Later my cooperating teacher cautioned me not to let the members of that group manipulate me as she had seen them do in that class. She said that "death" was not one of the choices I had given them. I did not see this as a serious problem and felt that my cooperating teacher was perhaps a bit too control-conscious. My feeling was that the project was theirs and I believed the group should have as much power over the process and product as possible. I did, however, heed the warning about manipulation.

A few days later, the "death" group went off to another classroom to work out some ideas. Even Rick made suggestions that were considered. The group discussed other options and moved away from Rick's idea. Rick complained that the group didn't like his ideas and that he didn't count. I told him that his "hurt puppy routine" was not appropriate and that if he wanted his ideas to count, he had to convince the group. He did not react well to my comments and became more negative about the whole process.

Rick showed up for only one of the next five classes, the day of performance. He thought that he should be allowed to perform, but the other members had voted him out the day before. I was glad to see them stick to their decision.

Working with this class taught me a lot about group dynamics. When Rick was not around, there were very few problems; the group worked very creatively with only minor guidance from me. I realized that Rick was so hurt inside that he literally sucked positive energy out of a group. I could also see that he used sexual undertones to manipulate the females. I do not believe the girls realized what Rick was doing, but from my standpoint it was very obvious.

What do you do with a student like Rick? My first impulse was to remove him from the class. But shouldn't I work with all the kids in my class? I do not have a good answer to this question. I was lucky that Rick chose not to come to class, making my job a lot easier. My cooperating teacher pointed out that teachers have to work with even the problem kids in order to maintain enrollment. One part of me says that removing serious problem students is a good choice because it allows the other kids to work in an environment that is more conducive to learning and growth. If problem students were to stay, they would drag the whole group down and those students who could really soar would be held back. On the other hand, I have the responsibility to give all students the opportunity to succeed.

Regardless, it is important to set up both my expectations and the boundaries for working. I think that when I told Rick that his victim routine was not working and that I expected him to work with his group, I was establishing some very significant boundaries. The group, in turn, held Rick accountable for his absence.

Everyone has boundaries, and those boundaries become obvious when they are tested. Some teacher boundaries will be directly expressed and some will come out naturally as part of the thousands of split-second decisions that teachers make. It is difficult to set up boundaries in a student teaching situation because the time period is so short. In addition, the student teacher enters a classroom where another set of boundaries are in place. I believe that we must give students the responsibility to create their own rules and live by them. Of course, the teacher must have a say in their creation. If my rules and consequences in my classroom had been laid out right from the start, maybe Rick would have learned how to work in the group, guided not only by the teacher but by the other students as well.

The Ricks of the world will not go away if we ignore them. We have to figure out a way for them to let go of their negativity and to work with the group in order for everyone to shine. This task is easier said than done; I must work at creating a classroom environment and culture in which kids like Rick can learn and grow.

A Student Teacher's Response: Now Is the Winter of Our Discontent: MaveRicks in the Classroom

This case clearly sets forth the dilemma that results from a basic question: As teachers, where do we draw the line with all the Ricks out there? How can we best modify their behaviors in such a way so they can remain part of the class and actually learn?

The most effective approach may involve sessions with Rick's parents; with a counselor/social worker; or one between teacher, principal, and Rick. Part of this work may extend beyond the immediate concerns of the individual teacher. And yet the drama teacher needs to be aware of Rick's problems and his progress in addressing them. This is especially important because of the experiential nature of drama work. Drama involves cooperation, communication, empathy, listening, and working in various kinds of groups. For a student with serious psychological problems, drama offers a great challenge and incredible opportunities related to affective education.

Affective education focuses on "mental health as evident in self-concept and self-esteem, human relationships and experiences, feelings and emotions, character, personality, personal philosophies, and personal and social adjustment" (Lang, McBeath, and Hebert 1995). Clearly, this is the domain of drama. Under the right conditions, substantive personal growth can occur in the drama classroom. Part of this growth can happen around the issue of boundaries. By facilitating the setting of clear, community-recognized boundaries in the classroom, the teacher can model a process of creating boundaries both for the individual and the group. If this process is openly discussed, then the group can have ownership of the standards of classroom culture.

The drama class can become a kind of laboratory for exploring values, behaviors, approaches, attitudes, and beliefs. Included here are the class rules, a natural and necessary part of a functioning community of learners rather than an edict from some authority figure. A delicate balance must be struck between the needs of the teacher and those of the students and also between the majority of students and certain individuals within the group. Teacher responsibility can then be weighed against student accountability on a daily, ongoing basis. Specific situations will require specific solutions, but now the teacher has a framework for handling the challenges of a Rick. By clearly stating the parameters of the classroom learning community, a teacher can give all those Ricks a clear choice and knowledge of the consequences that are in place. Students and teacher are thus mutually empowered: learning can proceed.

Some practical realities need to be considered. As the case suggests, this process of community building can be more difficult in practicum situations. Longer practicums (more than four weeks) are thus very useful for student teachers. Drama methods instructors could offer pointers to enhance effectiveness in short-term—and long-term—situations. Let's address trouble and its solutions so that we can become better prepared as educators.

A Teacher's Response: Boundaries in the Classroom

Should a classroom teacher attempt to work with the "problem" student even if it means the rest of the class may be held back? Teachers are often faced with such dilemmas: What is my responsibility to the student, and how do I weigh my responsibility to a single student against my responsibility to the entire class?

The student teacher was correct in pointing out the necessity of establishing boundaries. I also agree that students should take part in determining the boundaries. It has been my experience that, if students are given the responsibility of determining the guidelines operating in class, they will be much more likely to support them, or at least be understanding of consequences when those guidelines are violated.

I feel, however, that the student teacher undermined her or his own boundaries when she or he allowed a group of students to choose their own topic for a playbuilding project after having already assigned them the topic. I understand the reasoning: the teacher wanted the students to have ownership. However, the teacher had already discovered that Rick was one to push boundaries. This was the student teacher's opportunity to hold students to the guidelines that she or he had established. She or he failed to do this and it didn't bode well for Rick or the rest of the group.

Eventually the problem student stopped coming to class. There is a little irony here. Although the student teacher was very hesitant to remove Rick from the class, he or she felt relief when he stopped coming. We all can understand that feeling. When you realize that "that student" isn't in class today, you brighten a little and look forward to a good day.

I believe the conclusions that the student teacher reached are correct ones: laying out rules, guidelines, and consequences right from the start and creating a classroom culture in which students can learn and grow. In "MaveRicks in the Classroom," the writer suggests another effective solution. Sessions involving Rick's parents, administrators, and counselors might also be valuable. Of course, each student is an individual with unique problems. It is a teacher's responsibility to look for the solution that will be the most positive for all.

In my own practice, I have experienced students like Rick. Just this year I had a student whose behavior was very similar to that described by the student teacher. My student's first comment in class was that drama was for "faggots." This was the first of many derisive remarks uttered by David, and some were much more belligerent and disruptive to the class. I tried many responses: counseling, detentions and disciplinary referrals, phone calls home, and meetings with administrators. The student knew the guidelines and the consequences but still chose to be disruptive. The dilemma I had with this student was that every time I felt we were making progress, another outburst would occur. Eventually I had him removed from the class. I determined that he was too disruptive to the rest of the class when his behavior began to influence others. Since this was a beginning drama class, the students hadn't yet had the opportunity to establish the trust that is necessary. I saw David's behavior as a major impediment to that process.

As teachers we all can understand the situation in which this student teacher found her- or himself. We don't enjoy being placed in the predicament of having to weigh the risk to the class versus an individual's right to learn. However, if that situation occurs, the teacher owes it to all the persons involved to try to find the best solution and then act on it.

Extensions

1. The cooperating teacher gave the student teacher some background information on Rick's problems. What effect did this information have on the student teacher's observations and interventions? What might be the preconceptions underlying such information? How do we use background information in our teaching practice? How does it help us? Hinder us?

2. Other contextual information is given in this case, such as "This is a Catholic school." What assumptions might you make about the nature of a school based on this information? How would your assumptions change if the school were in an inner city or in a rural locale? Look at Posner's (1993) suggestions for understanding the school community in his book, *Field Experience.*

3. The student teacher allowed Rick's group to choose its their own topic. The cooperating teacher felt the student teacher had been manipulated by the students while the student teacher felt the cooperating teacher might be a little too control-conscious. What is the line between "teacher control" and "student control"? How would it help to think of both teaching and learning as a "working with," or collaborative situation?

4. The teacher's dilemma to remove a problem student is discussed by both the responding student teacher and the teacher. What do you consider to be the responsibilities of teachers, classmates, the school, and society to students like Rick?

5. In this case, the student teacher reports that Rick expressed violent fantasies in writing assignments. What legal responsibilities

do teachers have when they discover something like what Rick wrote? It is possible that Rick has some emotional disabilities. What sort of help is available to teachers when they encounter a student who may be emotionally disturbed?

REAL LIFE 101

In this case a high school faces a crisis when a popular student commits suicide.

The day that basketball player Magic Johnson announced to the world that he was HIV-positive was one of the worst days of my life. It was one of "those" days. You know the ones, like the day Kennedy was killed or the day the space shuttle exploded. Events such as these have such strong impacts that they seem trapped in time. Frozen. It is with this vivid clarity that I'm sure many students at the high school where I did my student teaching will remember the day when a very popular, respected student decided, for reasons only he will ever know, to commit suicide.

When I walked into the little theatre on this particular morning, I knew something was different. It wasn't just the thirty-some teachers holding a meeting in the theatre, either. It was their expressions, their gloom, as if a big, dark cloud was hanging over our school alone, leaving the rest of the world bright and sunny. I immediately caught on to the topic of the meeting. A student had committed suicide.

He was not a student in any of my classes, and when my cooperating teacher told me his name, it did not sound familiar. My immediate reaction, therefore, was that while this was an unfortunate tragedy, things like this happen. It happened at my high school when I was a student and it happens at some high school somewhere just about every day. I assumed this was most likely a student who was unpopular, who had few or no friends, and who was living an unhappy, confused home life. While the school would probably be shaken up over the event, we would band together and get over the loss.

It took me less than five minutes to realize I was wrong.

My beginning drama class started shortly after the emergency meeting. I was to announce first thing that there had been a suicide and that grief counselors were available in the library. Since this was second period, most of the students seemed to have heard about it already. Then I mentioned the student's name and asked the class if anyone knew him. This was the part I wasn't expecting; about thirty hands flew into the air followed by an avalanche of tears. Everything I had assumed about this particular student turned out to be wrong.

He was not a kid without friends, in fact he was almost a hero at school, and as far as I could tell, extremely well-liked. These qualities made the grieving process much more difficult to deal with.

Other than the information given to us in the brief meeting about thirty minutes earlier, I had nothing to go on. We were given a sheet of paper listing things that we should and should not say to our students and this quickly became my bible. The first thing we were advised to do was ask if anyone in the class had anything to say. Doing this, the paper said, would allow students to get any feelings they had bottled up out into the open. We were *not* supposed to say things like, "Get over it. Everyone has to die sometime," or "I know how you feel." Maybe it's just me, but this seemed kind of obvious. So, I did what the almighty sheet said to do. I gave up the floor.

One student, sitting right down in front, said that this particular student had been a friend of his, was a good guy, and would be missed. I didn't even have to ask if anyone else had anything to say. The first comment started the ball rolling. Almost everyone, it seemed, had something to say, and all were heartwarming and appropriate. I felt a great deal of admiration for these kids. They had lost a person who was apparently a very good friend and were handling it in a very adult manner. Some students were naturally more upset than others and some were downright devastated. I asked the class if anyone felt that he or she needed to go to the library, but no one did.

At this point I had to make a decision to either begin the planned lesson or to consider this a day off, as many other teachers were doing. I decided, after talking it over with my cooperating teacher, to forge ahead with a hands-on lighting workshop. I felt that this might temporarily take the students' minds off this tragedy. While a majority of the students were understandably quiet and somber, and while I may not have actually taught much that day, I feel that this proved to be the right decision.

The rest of that day and the three days that followed were truly an experience I won't soon forget—sometimes sad, sometimes frightening, sometimes angry, and always unpredictable. There were moments that were so quiet you could have heard a pin drop in the hallways and other times that music blared and students wailed their tributes. The intersection nearest the school was painted with big, louder-than-life messages, reaching the heavens to proclaim the students' love for their fallen hero. For three days the administration kept no attendance records, nor did they monitor the parking lots or attempt to control where the students were. They called an assembly to provide another outlet for student expression. The school, in my opinion, did a wonderful job coping with this situation, which was a damn good thing, because I was lost.

I finally decided to continue with the lessons that I had planned for the rest of the week. While this sometimes proved difficult, I think that everything ended up okay in the long run. We managed to help work through the strong emotions by giving the students a little space and freedom, and my students did fairly well on their lighting tests.

How does one deal with such an incredible event? I was taught plenty of things in my education classes such as managing discipline problems and adjusting lesson plans to accommodate students with special needs. I've compared learning students to salivating dogs; I've learned the ins and outs of ADHD; and I've had entire classes with professors telling me exactly how the adolescent mind operates. But never once had anyone told me how people cope with suicide. It's too bad I never had Real Life 101. I can't tell you how to deal with this type of situation now, although I've been through it. I can generalize and tell you what seemed to work well, but I don't expect this situation to ever be exactly replicated. What I can tell you is this: know your classroom; know your students, and let them know you care.

A Student Teacher's Response: Living with Death

Teenage suicide raises questions of life and death. The greatest challenge a teacher might face is how its occurrence can affect our students. The event itself proves to be traumatic, but the search for answers, and the role of a teacher caught in the middle, is really what this powerful case is all about.

The news of the untimely death of a popular student turned the high school on its head. Death is a topic not usually addressed in schools until it presents itself. The student teacher's position is complicated by his or her unfamiliarity with this situation, one not found in textbooks. Fortunately, the administration responded immediately, providing teachers with guidelines and students with support. I was impressed with the student teacher's decision to continue the scheduled lesson. Sometimes the best way to deal with loss is to continue with regular daily activities, allowing time and space to grieve.

Ultimately, what we do as teachers and parents is try to help young people understand that it is not that a person dies that makes a difference, but that a person lives.

A Teacher's Response: What Is Teacher "Preparation"?

This case raises the issue of how well educational institutions prepare their teachers and students for the unpredictable events that occur in schools. Because of the recent outbreaks of anger and violence, especially in today's classrooms, this issue is of critical importance. Experience is telling us that we are not prepared. To help resolve this situation, all levels of the educational community should become involved in proactive methods and practices to deal with a variety of possible circumstances including earthquakes, suicide, threats, harassment, weapons, etc.

Fortunately, in this instance, the student teacher was provided with a process for dealing with the suicide before meeting the students. Unfortunately, however, there does not appear to have been any preliminary work done in this or other potentially volatile areas that may have prepared the student teacher. Are any of us ever prepared for the unknown?

I wonder how prepared I am as an administrator and educator in dealing with the myriad of potentially dangerous, volatile, and emotional roller coasters that can prevail in any school. As I write this response, I am guilty of feeling lucky that I have not experienced any disastrous events in my career. At the same time, I feel extremely negligent in not preparing myself, let alone others, for the unknown! One would agree that this school handled the situation, but the effort was reactive rather than proactive. Drama education is an excellent context in which to teach students and faculty how to deal with real-life situations and I would encourage such education to be required/compulsory for all.

Extensions

1. The literature on suicide describes warning signals. What are these? What should/could/would you do if one of your students displayed these symptoms? What kind of support can you expect from your administration? What is your school policy regarding crisis management?
2. Some people believe that mentioning problems illicits unnecessary grief; others say that talking about a recent suicide might cause a copycat death. What is your opinion? Research teen suicide to find other perspectives.
3. The student teacher decided to continue with the lighting lesson as planned. Make a list of other activities he or she might have done in this situation.

THE PLACES I WENT

A female student teacher describes her harassment by a male student.

When I first embarked on this journey to become a teacher, there were definitely places that I wanted to go. It has not been as easy as I originally thought. My second day at Community High School was the first domino in the chain of events that would most affect me as a student teacher.

Besides teaching drama I also taught a lower-level English class—a seemingly harmless placement. The students in this particular class were deemed by the administration to be "unmotivated, unskilled," and therefore "untrainable." Many of the students had had multiple failures in English and came from troubled backgrounds. They had previously been through the same curriculum, without success. In the classroom they were very unmotivated and they tended to "act up." The resulting suspensions only served to put the students further behind academically.

A male student with a chronic attendance problem had been absent on Monday, so Tuesday was my first meeting with him. He was, at nineteen, only one year younger than I and was attempting this course for the fourth time. Tom was quite an intense individual, and, I, being young, single, and female, immediately felt awkward around him. Halfway through the first period, I noticed Tom, another male student, and one female student laughing and making obscene gestures in the back of the room. Since my cooperating teacher was in the middle of a lesson, I moved to intercede. As I got closer, I was able to hear parts of the conversation, which was about oral sex and was directed at the female student. When I confronted all three on what I had heard and seen, Tom took his "cue," and the power visibly began to shift.

Immediately my sexuality was called into question. Was I jealous? Would I enjoy such acts? Tom speculated that I would and was probably experienced in such matters. Shocked, I called attention to the inappropriateness of the situation and made a break for the safety of the front of the room.

Luckily, my peer in this dual placement had witnessed the entire event, and I was able to discuss it with her and our cooperating teacher. This prompted our cooperating teacher to go to the administration with yet another complaint against Tom. It turned out that this would be *the* incident to finally expel him. Despite his previous four years of accumulated yellow slips, it was this act of sexual harassment that the administration believed would be most effective.

Three days into my practicum I appeared at Tom's expulsion hearing, giving sworn statements in front of the predominately male school board. It was painful to have my every word, action, gesture, and piece of clothing put under a microscope. Initially, the board supported me, but unfortunately, this support was short-lived. Tom's parents contacted a lawyer who claimed that the school's accusations were damaging to Tom's character and threatened legal action. Ten days later, I was shocked to find Tom back in my class, sitting and grinning up at me! After a process that excluded many of us most affected, it was decided that Tom would return to my classroom and continue with his education. This was the lowest point of my entire practicum. Tom's rights seemed to overshadow mine and I felt unprotected and very alone.

The political and bureaucratic sides of education were beginning to make me bitter. I began to resent the students as well as the administration. I lost my passion for teaching and despite the successes I had achieved on many levels, I felt that I was a failure. I spent as much time planning ways of not making myself vulnerable as I did planning ways to teach the curriculum. I knew that what I was accomplishing in the classroom was not a true representation of my abilities. I began to question my decision to teach.

I became extremely depressed. I stopped sleeping through the night and became agitated. I cried for a straight week and sought counseling. I needed a break from school. Although my parents were extremely supportive—my father is a teacher/administrator—as were my cooperating teacher and my methods instructor, I felt very little support elsewhere. The field experience office at the university seemed confused as to what to do. The school administration was sheepish and most likely embarrassed by the outcome. I trusted the school to protect me and felt let down. I was frightened and remained on edge throughout the practicum.

I began to move from self-examination to self-blame. I evaluated and reevaluated myself. I was afraid to go out at night with my friends, as many of my students were old enough to frequent the same nightclubs. On one occasion, Tom found out where I was going and, unbeknownst to me, showed up there. The following Monday in class he told me what I had worn, drank, and done. Once again I called the university field experience office and contacted the police; however, no action was taken. I was convinced that I had somehow asked for this to happen because I was a young, single female naively thinking that I could effectively teach in a high school. I just wanted to finish my practicum quickly.

In looking back, I am trying to understand other factors that might have contributed to this situation. Because of his multiple failures, Tom was a much older student than his classmates and his sense of belonging hinged on him being laid-back, cool, and a risk taker. He had nothing to lose by confronting me in front of his peers and everything to gain through the attention he would receive. He also needed to build up his self-esteem by being able to diminish the power I had over him. Despite the fact that I was only one year older than Tom, I had already completed three years toward a university degree, while he was still struggling with grade 10 material. No wonder Tom viewed me with hostility. I was a constant reminder of what he was not—an enormous threat to his self-esteem.

I should not have gotten into the power struggle with Tom. I should have removed Tom from his peers as soon as a challenge was issued. This would have prevented him from getting the attention he was seeking, while allowing me to maintain a professional dignity in the eyes of my students. However, these conclusions in no way excuse what Tom did. As a legal adult, his actions were criminal and I could have formally pressed charges. He knew that what he was saying was inappropriate in any context. The fact that I was his teacher only compounded an already-serious problem. Despite any questions or regrets I may have about my experience with Tom, I wholeheartedly stand by my choices and professional decorum toward him.

I still have places that I would like to go in my teaching career. Prior to the practicum, I knew where those places were, or at least I thought I did. Now, I haven't a clue as to the direction that I'm heading. But at least I'm still going.

A Student Teacher's Response: Safety in the Workplace

As a future student teacher, I question the school's wisdom to place a young teacher in an English class for "unmotivated, unskilled," and "untrainable" students. These students would be a challenge for an expert teacher, let alone a novice. Does the school want to promote a positive student teaching experience or does it just hope the student teacher survives? This student teacher's lack of confidence and youthful appearance worked against her in this situation and led her down a path of stress and depression. She began to question whether teaching was an appropriate profession for her. It takes a very strong person to remain in a situation when she or he must dread entering the classroom on a daily basis. For this, I commend her.

This situation clearly could have been handled better by the school's administration. It was extremely unprofessional for the school to allow Tom back into the student teacher's classroom without forewarning her. For a young woman, sexual harassment is frightening and belittling. The school administration did not take this situation seriously enough. Administrators also excluded her from the decision-making process that would impact both her and Tom. It might have been better if Tom or the student teacher could have been relocated to a different classroom. As she pointed out, the students' rights were more protected than hers.

This case also brings up the issue of safety in the workplace. How well do schools protect teachers from students who threaten and harass them? Do teachers have a panic button they can push if there is an emergency? Are other teachers around to act as witnesses during a confrontation like the one this student teacher had? What preparation are teachers given to handle situations regarding sexual harassment and intimidation? Teachers have to control the balance of power between them and their students, not vice versa, and they have a right themselves to feel safe in their own classrooms.

A Teacher's Response: You Shouldn't Have to Travel Alone

The central issue of "The Places I Went" involves the roles and responsibilities of the cooperating teacher and school administration. The very fact that "four years of accumulated yellow slips" wasn't enough documentation to have a nineteen-year-old student with obvious behavior problems removed from the school is evidence enough that the school administration had not effectively dealt with the problems associated with this particular student. The school, it seems, jumped at the chance that the harassment incident provided and required this inexperienced, young female to testify in front of the school board, where she was questioned, scrutinized, and eventually victimized by school board bureaucracy. Thus, the long journey began. . . .

While it was morally reprehensible for the student teacher to be excluded from the decision-making process that reinstated Tom in the school, even more outrageous is the fact that this teacher was expected to *continue* to teach him. Through the remainder of the practicum, she was forced to endure ongoing incidents of harassment and stalking. In this case, it is clear that the rights of one student overshadowed the rights of his teacher.

If the school administration wanted this student teacher's testimony, more thought and planning should have gone into the process. The school administrators and the cooperating teacher had the responsibility to ensure that the student teacher would be treated in a dignified manner regardless of the outcome. This means having a contingency plan in effect. When it became obvious that the male student was going to return to school, steps should have been taken to ensure that the student teacher would not be put in the awkward position of having to teach him.

Although the cooperating teacher was described as supportive, the case does not describe the ways in which the cooperating teacher acted as an advocate for the student teacher. Certainly when it became clear that the harassment was going to continue, a quick response from the cooperating teacher, school administration, and/or field experience office could have prevented further difficulties.

How can student teachers learn from the unfortunate experiences described in this case? First of all, I believe that all student teachers need to become informed of their roles, rights, and responsibilities. Clearly, the student teacher was put in a difficult situation well beyond her job description. Perhaps she should have voiced her concerns sooner. Conversely, cooperating teachers, school administrators, teacher unions, and universities need to work in partnership to ensure that all stakeholders within the education system have a voice. I believe that student teachers are often "silenced." They fear that intervention or asking for support will be interpreted as weakness and will affect the outcome of their evaluation and future job prospects.

To ensure a positive experience, lines of communication must be kept open. Student teachers need to work in partnership with their cooperating teachers to solve difficult challenges as they arise. Student teachers are not certified teachers and should not be afraid to ask questions, seek support, or ask for guidance. Additionally, the cooperating teacher has a responsibility to foster a supportive learning environment by offering advice and assistance and even acting as an advocate for the student teacher.

The fact that the student teacher was able to reflect on the situation and salvage some learning from the whole experience shows that she has the skills and potential to become a very good teacher. It is unfortunate that this experience served to alienate her from her ideals and reasons for becoming a teacher in the first place. She was forced to travel a difficult journey.

Extensions

1. Harassment is a serious problem in schools. What are your legal responsibilities in your state or province should you witness harass-

ment of any sort? Find out from your cooperating teacher what the policy is at your placement school. Discuss with your university advisor what you should do if you witness threats or are threatened in any way.

2. The teacher's response suggests that student teachers become aware of their rights as well as their responsibilities. Find out what your legal rights are in the classroom. This information is usually available from the university field placement office. What professional memberships are available to you in your university, state or province, or country? What might be the benefits to you as a student teacher in joining such an organization?

3. Set up a forum theatre (Boal 1979) situation that is similar to the confrontation the student teacher experienced with Tom. What can you learn from this activity?

7

The Student Teaching Experience

HELP, I'M BECOMING A TEACHER

The student teacher in this case discusses the transformation from student to teacher.

Learning to teach is an emotional roller coaster. A lesson goes well with one class but doesn't get finished in another. Student comments such as "This isn't drama" make my blood boil! On the other hand, small things like a student saying after class, "Those masks are neat!" make all the difference. I have heard teachers say that it is the little things that make teaching worthwhile. I believed them, but I didn't really understand it on a cognitive level until my practicum. This has been just one of my many ultimate realizations about teaching.

I spent every morning, eighty minutes a day, with a grade 10 class. Legend has it that last year, when these students were in grade 9, they got 80 percent of all school suspensions in the school district. So it stood to reason that I would have a few difficult students in this class. Because there were also students who were taking the class for an easy grade, some of them believed there would not be any writing, reading, or exams. When I introduced a play study unit and a written journal (providing questions for graded response), they tried everything to undermine this procedure, such as coming to class without paper or pens. Their favorite complaint was "This is drama, not English!" I would say, "This is drama, a course like any other course, and it is recognized by the admissions committee of any university!" What I really wanted to say was, "Be quiet and do as you're told with no more complaints!" I did finally say, "These are the things you are required to know at the end of the course and this is how you will learn them!" I have a teaching style! Another realization.

I loved my grade 12 class because the students really wanted to learn about drama; they appreciated what I had to offer and listened to my suggestions. Though this sounds like a total ego boost, which I suppose it was to some extent, what I really mean to say is that it was refreshing to talk to students who responded positively. I spent a number of hours working with individuals as they prepared their monologues for class presentation. One of the students was working on a monologue titled "Help I'm Becoming My Mother." This was a quirky piece employing understated humor. Her presentation went very well, accompanied by as much appropriate laughter as can be expected of students who have not encountered the agony of realizing they are *just like their mothers.* Anyway, the words of this monologue floated through my mind at the oddest times.

I had gone to the photocopy room to find that the copy machine was on the fritz—again. I went to the staff room to attend a Friday staff meeting and heard the physical education department praised—again; the news that another eighty computers were to be installed the following week, making the total five hundred and forty; and a reminder to teachers on lunch duty to please facilitate garbage pickup.

I realized I had put my keys down in the copy room. Backtracking, I arrived, found a piece of string, strung the keys around my neck, and returned to the drama lab. When I passed the wall of shopping mall–type mirrors, I caught a glimpse of myself. I did a double take to confirm what I had just seen. There I stood, in comfortable shoes and respectable, somewhat understated clothes, with a box full of "materials" under one arm, a coffee cup in the other hand, and my keys, purple dinosaur key chain and all, tied with a string around my neck! The words of that monologue came to mind: "Help me, I'm becoming a teacher!" Realization number three.

I sat for a while, disturbed by the whole experience. This did not seem like me, at least not the "me" that I had become accustomed to. I know inside that I am still the same person, yet now, I have firsthand knowledge of the everyday stresses of being a teacher. Each time I look at the staff parking sticker on my car, I'm reminded that I have taken the first steps into the exclusive order of teachers.

I can't quite accept the keys around the neck, though—they *must* go. Teacher or . . . not!

A Student Teacher's Response: From Student to Teacher—You Are What You Wear!

Reading this case made me realize that self-reflection can be really helpful, especially if you take note of what is going on and decide whether you need to change your approach. Reflections also help you realize what kind of teacher you are becoming.

This case looks humorously at the student teacher's discoveries about teaching. When he or she stopped to reflect on his or her practicum, he or she realized that he or she was no longer rehearsing the role of teacher: she or he had become a teacher, costume and all!

A Teacher's Response: Those Wonderful "Ultimate Realizations"

Reading this case made me both wistful and elated. Why wistful? As I read through this teacher's journey, I was reminded of the times I experienced the same "Ah ha!" moments.

Throughout this teacher's career, as in my own, there will be reminders that no matter how gloomy a particular class or lesson may have been there is that "little thing" that makes coming back to class the next day worthwhile. It may be the moment of insight in a student's eyes, the pleasure taken in a response, or the quiet comment demonstrating interest and appreciation.

There will also be those recurring moments when, as teachers, we take a firm stand by making clear our expectations and the direction we wish the class to follow, all because we believe in what we want to communicate and we know the ultimate, implicit value.

Lastly, there are those days when we come together with our students in the sheer joy of sharing and expressing our love for the material. These are "over-the-top" moments that reaffirm for all teachers the joy of teaching activated through a shared love of learning.

I am elated for this new teacher. I celebrate, as a colleague, her or his realizations; they bind us together in the "exclusive order of teachers."

As to the keys . . . I have used a florescent, stretchy coil on the wrist.

Extensions

1. During your practicum, you may find yourself disconnected from your familiar world and support system. Suddenly you are no longer part of college life, but you are not really a member of the school community, either. When you student teach, what can you do to maintain your familiar support systems?

2. Many new demands will be made of you during your practicum; for example, you will be preparing lessons daily sometimes for multiple

classes and grading student work in a timely fashion. Interacting with a hundred or more teenagers on a daily basis may also place new strains on you. What stress management techniques can you use during your practicum? How can you ensure that you eat and sleep properly and to take time out for yourself?

3. One of the keys to stress management is good time management. How would you assess your time management skills? How can you improve time management during your practicum?

Afterword
Moving Beyond Telling and Listening to Stories

As I read and reread this manuscript, I reflected on how the stories that the authors call case narratives can be used in different ways in teacher education classes. Each way, depending on the vantage point of the reader, offers possibilities for understanding more about storied knowledge, what we call personal practical knowledge as composed and lived out on storied landscapes.

The book reminds me of how powerful all of us, including preservice teachers, find writing our own teaching stories to be. I use story writing in my preservice and graduate level classes, and students invariably tell me how much they learn about themselves from this process. As they compose, write, and read their stories, they come to new realizations about how they both live and tell their stories of themselves as teachers. I imagine that the preservice teachers who shared their stories in these pages experienced something similar. Learning to tell your own stories and learning from reading them points to one way to use this book: as a way to encourage all preservice teachers to tell their stories.

But this book pushes past learning to tell our own stories and begins to play at the edges of response. In the book, other readers, positioned in other places on the landscape, responded to each story. The first readers, preservice teachers, responded to the stories, occasionally laying one of their own stories alongside the first story. The second readers, experienced teachers, also responded to the stories. As I read their responses, I was encouraged to go back and reread the story, sometimes startled by how differently I read the stories than did the other readers. I learned not only from my first reading but from the second reading. I learned also from thinking about why I might have read the story so differently than another reader did. This is another way to use the stories in teacher education classes: reading the stories, writing our responses to them, reading responses from others, rereading the stories yet again for new interpretations and understandings.

The book helps us see that when we tell one of our stories, the response makes a difference in what we can see in our story. I imagine, for example, that the diverse responses made a difference to the student teacher who wrote "Eliminating the Creature, Embracing the Creature." She or he chose to tell the story around a plotline of learning how students with unique narrative histories come to the spaces and activities we, as teachers, structure for them. Their unique narrative histories shape how they experience instructional events. That story was read by two readers who each responded differently. These different responses remind us of the power of multiple responses and the lived experience each reader brings to a text. We each listen to, and read, stories differently. We make meaning depending upon our narratives of experience, how we are positioned on the landscape, the time, the spaces we are in at the time of reading, and so forth. Different stories call forth different responses. We can learn something new about our stories from each diverse response.

Sometimes responses are storied ones. Our stories call up other stories in response and we learn from this interactive approach. While the responses in the book are not storied ones, we gain a sense of possible stories that each reader might have told in response. The teacher's response to "Real Life 101" gives a sense of how he or she is living his or her life. The teacher acknowledges that he or she is uncertain about how prepared he or she is. The teacher wonders if he or she can ever be prepared. His or her own story of uncertainty opens up different possible interpretations for the storyteller. Imagine, for a moment, how a story with a plotline of uncertainty in response to the teller's story would open up a conversation about wide awakeness, about teaching as improvisation, about relational knowing with students. Such a storied response helps show us the possibility for education, for growth, in those imagined subsequent conversations.

There is yet another way to use this book, a way that allows us to begin to move past the telling of stories to the retelling and reliving of stories. In the book we do not see how the story writers were changed by the responses. I wondered if they would have changed how they told, and might relive, their stories after engaging with the responses of others. Writing stories and receiving response to them offers educative possibilities. I often structure teacher education classes to provide time for students to write their stories and then to share them in response communities. In such communities, students have the chance to write their stories, receive response to them, and begin to retell their stories. In these response communities, stories do not become something fixed and unchanging but are always stories in progress, open to change and reinterpretation. This is where the most possibility lies for teacher education, that is, when it becomes clear that all of us are always in the midst of composing our stories of teaching. Our stories are always open to revision in the telling, retelling, and reliving of them. Through this process our knowing, as teachers, is storied and then restoried. Although this is not made explicit in the telling and responding to stories in these pages, the book shows us how we might provide this opportunity for students in our preservice classes.

When Joe Norris asked if I would write the afterword for this book, he told me the story he shares in the introduction to this book, in which he recalls another teacher's story while he tries to relate to a room of junior high school students. The remembered story offers Joe a possible plotline to live out with the students. It works when he tries it out. The first story leads to another story, Joe's story. In the book Joe lays his story beside the first teacher's story. As we read the stories in this book, they will, for each of us, call up other stories. This laying of our stories side by side is what Janice Huber (2000) and Karen Whelan (2000) call narrative interlapping. It is in these narrative interlapping spaces that we can tell, retell, and possibly begin to relive new stories. This book furthers our thinking about the ways in which stories help us reach new understandings and new possibilities in teacher education.

D. Jean Clandinin, *University of Alberta*

Appendix A:
The Case Study Assignment

Rationale: The case study is an attempt to link the student teaching practicum and university courses more closely together. Your case will be drawn directly from an experience during your final field experience.

Method: Describe a significant challenge, professional growth, incident, concern, or issue you have encountered in your field experience and write this as a formal case study.

- What is your concern?
- When did you first notice it?
- What specific actions did you take as a result of this concern?
- What were the differences or discrepancies in the way this concern ended in comparison to the way you had originally intended or thought this situation would end?
- Were you surprised with the result? Why or why not?
- How will this experience influence your future teaching?

Suggestions for Beginning:

- You are encouraged to keep a journal of your daily experiences during the student teaching practicum. Classroom incidents, writing, discussion with students, student teacher, or cooperating teachers could be data for a case study. Since you might not initially perceive an incident as a potential case study, a journal will record events for later analysis. Make a daily list of thoughts about how your day/week is going. Be concrete by providing specific examples.
- Continually reread your list, making notes of emerging themes or patterns.
- Choose one that seems to be the most significant for you and begin writing about it. You may wish to discuss your thoughts with

your cooperating teacher and design some specific actions required as a result of your reflections.

- Relook at your class notes and readings and relate your case to the theory/issues covered in class.
- Changing the topic and/or exploring more than one topic can be an appropriate strategy.
- Be prepared to discuss your case work during the last three weeks of this semester. We will use your information as a basis for class discussions and instruction. This should assist you in refining your thoughts on your practicum experience.

Guidelines for Writing Your Case:

1. Begin with your description of the case itself. Be sure to include whatever background information a reader might need to fully follow your case. Write the case in the first person. Case studies can be written about others, but the nature of this course is to provide you with some reflective practice experience. This case must be about you in some way. All names must be pseudonyms.
2. After you have completed a description of the events in the case, include a reflective analysis of the issue(s) utilizing resources from ALL your education course work and other relevant experiences. This is your opportunity to integrate learning from all your previous educational experiences.
3. Apply your experience and insights to future practice.
4. Choose a creative title to frame your case.
5. Your case study is expected to be from eight to ten typed, double-spaced pages.

Appendix B:
Responding to the Case Study

The purpose of these discussions is to help you to experience the world of teaching drama by vicariously sharing in the experiences of others. As you read the case, take note of the major issues facing the student teacher in the case, asking yourself:

1. What do I know about the events in the case?
2. What am I assuming about the events in the case?
3. What would I like to know about the situation in the case?

These three questions will help you keep to the details of the case.

As you discuss, first try to briefly summarize the case, pointing out the educational issues behind the events. These will be things that are experienced by many who teach and deserve considerable thought. Second, analyze both the events and the issues. Relate them to educational literature, class discussions, and your own personal experiences. Remember, however, that the cases are contextual and dependent upon teaching/learning styles that may not be evident in the case. You may hypothesize what you might have done using the magic of "what if," but be cautious of saying what the case writer "should have done." Finally, summarize your insights by making some concrete suggestions to yourself regarding what you might specifically do when you teach. For example, you may start off generally stating "I will become more friendly," but this alone is not enough. Making a list of specific activities like "greet students at the door with a smile," "personally hand out all assignments," "set office hours and 'invite' students to come in" may be useful. These will move you into action. You may even end up devising a lesson plan that will address your thoughts. Remember to critique these actions as well, examining what is problematic (creates problems) about them.

Remember that the case to which you are responding was written by someone who was/is trying to understand his or her place in this complex profession called "teaching." She or he has offered it to the public so that he or she and we can learn from these experiences. Respond to these cases keeping the tone of professionalism required for this collaborative venture.

Appendix C: Case Study Permission for Usage

I recognize that a Case Study, besides being a useful personal resource, can be a resource for those who follow after me. It provides a context of a "real" person trying to function in a "real" situation, albeit from one individual's perspective. Regardless, it can serve as a trigger for discussion and as an exemplar for future Case Studies.

I further recognize that, as I have benefited from the experiences of those students who have gone before me, I have the professional responsibility to pass on some of my work for others to build on.

I hereby give (methods instructor's name) permission to (Indicate Yes/No on each line):

_____ use my Case Study in its entirety in her/his classes to generate discussion and to be used as an exemplar.

_____ to pass on my Case Study in its entirety to other instructors to be utilized in their classes to generate discussion and to be used as an exemplar.

_____ use portions of my Case Study for his/her research into the use of the Case Study Method.

_____ use portions of my Case Study for her/his research of the student teaching experience.

_____ use portions of my Case Study for his/her research on the teaching of drama.

_____ use my Case Study in a book of Case Studies. I understand that this work, if chosen, will be accompanied by responses written by members in the field of drama education.

I understand that the names of the people whom I have described and myself will remain confidential but that a general acknowledgment of student contributors will be made.

_____

Name (please print):

_____

Signature

_____

Date

Bibliography

WORKS CITED

Atkinson, R. 1995. *The Gift of Stories: Practical and Spiritual Applications of Autobiography, Life Stories, and Personal Mythmaking.* Westport, CT: Bergin & Garvey.

Barone, T. 1990. "Using the Narrative Text as an Occasion for Conspiracy." In *Qualitative Inquiry in Education,* ed. E. W. Eisner & A. Peshkin, 305–26. New York: Teachers College Press.

Boal, A. 1979. *Theatre of the Oppressed.* London: Pluto Press.

Cangelosi, J. S. 1999. *Classroom Management Strategies: Gaining and Maintaining Students' Cooperation.* 4th ed. White Plains, NY: Longman.

Cell, E. 1984. *Learning to Learn from Experience.* Albany, NY: State University of New York Press.

Chapin, H. 1978. "Flowers Are Red." In *A Legacy in Song.* New York: Cherry Lane Music Company.

Charles, C. M., G. W. Senter, and K. B. Barr. 1999. *Building Classroom Discipline.* 6th ed. New York: Longman.

Clandinin, D., A. Davies, P. Hogan, and B. Kennard. 1993. *Learning to Teach and Teaching to Learn: Stories of Collaboration in Teacher Education.* New York: Teachers College Press.

Clarke, J., W. Dobson, T. Goode, and J. Neelands. 1997. *Lessons for the Living: Drama in the Transition Years.* Markham, ON: Mayfair Cornerstone.

Denzin, N. K. 1989. *Interpretive Biography.* Newbury Park, CA: Sage Publications.

Donmoyer, R. 1990. "Generalizability and the Single-Case Study." In *Qualitative Inquiry in Education,* ed. E. W. Eisner & A. Peshkin, 175–200. New York: Teachers College Press.

Geertz, C. 1974. "From the Native's Point of View: On the Nature of Anthropological Understanding." In *Interpretive Social Sciences,* ed. P. Rabinow & W. Sullivan. Berkeley, CA: University of California Press.

Innocenti, R. 1990. *Rose Blanche.* New York: Stewart, Tabori, & Chang, Inc.

115

Huber, J. 2000. *Stories Within and Betwen Selves: Identities in Relation on the Professional Knowledge Landscape.* Unpublished doctoral dissertation. University of Alberta.

Kempe, A. 1994. *Drama Sampler: Preparations and Presentations for First Drama.* Gloucester, England: Stanley Thomas.

———. 1996. *Drama Education and Special Needs.* Cheltenham, UK: Stanley Thornes.

———. 1997. *Starting with Scripts.* Cheltenham, UK: Stanley Thornes.

Kingsolver, B. 1995. *High Tide in Tucson.* New York: Harper Collins.

Lang, H., A. McBeath, and J. Hebert. 1995. *Teaching Strategies and Methods for Student-Centered Instruction.* Toronto, ON: Harcourt Brace.

Lundy, C., and D. Booth. 1983. *Interpretation.* Toronto, ON: Harcourt, Brace, Jovanovich.

Maslow, A. 1970. *Motivation and Personality.* New York: Harper and Row.

Morgan, N., and J. Saxton. 1987. *Teaching Drama: A Mind of Many Wonders.* London: Hutchinson.

———. 1991. *Asking Better Questions.* Markham, ON: Pembroke.

Nachmanovitch, S. 1990. *Free Play: The Power of Improvisation in Life and the Arts.* Los Angeles: Jeremy Tarcher Inc.

Neelands, J. 1984. *Making Sense of Drama.* London: Heinemann.

———. 1990. *Structuring Drama Work.* New York: Cambridge University Press.

Noddings, N. 1984. *Caring: A Feminine Approach to Ethics and Moral Education.* Berkeley, CA: University of California Press.

Norris, J. 1995. "Response-Able Guided Imagery." *Stage of the Art* 7(4): 4–9.

O'Neill, C., & A. Lambert. 1982. *Drama Structures.* Portsmouth, NH: Heinemann.

O'Neill, C., A. Lambert, R. Linnell, and J. Warr-Wood. 1976. *Drama Guidelines.* London: Heinemann Educational Books.

Parsons, J., and L. Beauchamp. 1990. *Stories of Teaching.* Richmond Hill, VA: Scholastic Press.

Pavio, A. 1971. *Imagery and Verbal Processes.* New York: Holt, Rinehart, and Winston.

Peter, M. 1994. *Drama for All: Developing Drama in the Curriculum for Students with Special Needs.* London: Fulton.

———. 1995. *Making Drama Special.* London: David Fulton.

Posner, G. 1993. *Field Experience: A Guide to Reflective Teaching.* New York: Longman.

Richler, M. 1959. *The Apprenticeship of Duddy Kravitz.* Toronto, ON: McLelland and Stewart.

Shulman, J., ed. 1992. *Case Methods in Teacher Education.* New York: Teachers College Press.

Shulman, J., and J. A. Colbert. 1988. *The Intern Teacher Casebook.* San Francisco: Far West Laboratory for Educational Research and Development.

Shulman, J., and A. Mesa-Bains. 1993. *Diversity in the Classroom: A Casebook for Teachers and Teacher Educators.* Hillsdale, NJ: Research for Better Schools and Lawrence Erlbaum Association.

Shulman, L. 1993. "To Reinvent a Pedagogy for Teacher Education." Paper presented at the Western Canadian Conference for Student Teaching, Vancouver, BC.

Tarlington, C., and W. Michaels. 1995. *Building Plays: Simple Playbuilding Techniques at Work.* Markham, ON: Pembroke.

Wagner, B. J. 1976. *Dorothy Heathcote: Drama as a Learning Medium.* Washington: National Education Association.

Warner, C. 1998. "Constructing a Picasso: The Significance of Teacher Engagement." *Nadie Journal* 22(1): 39–44.

Whelan, K. 2000. *Stories of Self and Other: Identities in Relation on the Professional Knowledge Landscape.* Unpublished doctoral dissertation, The University of Alberta.

SUGGESTED READINGS

Case Study and Reflective Practice

Black, R., and K. Jones. 1996. *Writing Case Studies: A Holistic Approach for Teaching Preservice Educators About Students with Disabilities.* Cincinnati, OH: American Vocational Association Convention. ERIC Document Reproduction Service No. ED 404 489.

Clark, C., and S. Florio-Ruane. 1990. "Using Case Studies to Enrich Field Experience." *Teacher Education Quarterly* 17(1): 17–28.

Connelly, E., and D. Clandinin. 1988. *Teachers as Curriculum Planners: Narratives of Experience.* Toronto, ON: OISE Press.

Cooper, J. 1995. *Teacher's Problem Solving: A Casebook of Award-Winning Teaching Cases.* Toronto, ON: Allyn & Bacon.

Florio-Ruane, S. 1990. "Creating Your Own Case Studies: A Guide for Early Field Experience." *Teacher Education Quarterly* 17(1): 29–41.

Garrison, J., and H. Harrington. 1992. "Cases as Shared Inquiry: A Dialogical Model of Teacher Preparation." *American Educational Research Journal* 29(4): 715–35.

Goldsberry, L., and R. Mayer. 1993. "Searching for Reflection in the Student Teaching Experience: Two Case Studies." *Teacher Education Quarterly* 20(1): 13–27.

Hansen, A. 1997. "Writing Cases for Teaching: Observations of a Practitioner." *Kappan* 78(5): 398–403.

Hare, W. 1993. "The Nature and Value of Case Studies." In *What To Do?: Case Studies for Teachers,* ed. W. Hare and J. P. Portelli, 19–31. Halifax, NS: Fairmount Books.

Henderson, J. 1992. *Reflective Teaching: Becoming an Inquiring Educator.* Toronto, ON: Maxwell Macmillan Canada.

Henson, K. 1988. "Case Study in Teacher Education." *Educational Forum* 52(3): 235–41.

Huyvaert, S. 1995. *Reports from the Classroom.* Toronto, ON: Allyn & Bacon.

Kasten, B., and J. Write. 1996. *Engaging Preservice Teachers in Collaborative Inquiry Through the Development of Individual Case Studies.* St. Louis, MO: Association of Teacher Educators. ERIC Document Reproduction Service No. ED 395908.

Kauffman, J. M., D. P. Hallanhan, M. P. Mostert, S. C. Trent, and D. G. Nuttycombe. 1993. *Managing Classroom Behavior: A Reflective Case-Based Approach.* Boston: Allyn & Bacon.

Kemmis, S., and R. McTaggart. 1988. *The Action Research Planner.* Geelong, Victoria, Austalia: Deacon University Press.

Kleinfeld, J. 1990. "The Special Virtues of the Case Method in Preparing Teachers for Minority Schools." *Teacher Education Quarterly* 17(1): 43–51.

Kleinfeld, J., and N. Steiger, eds. 1991. *On a White Horse: Teaching Cases in Cross-Cultural Education.* No. 8. Fairbanks, AL: Alaska University Center for Cross-Cultural Studies. ERIC Document Reproduction Service No. ED 344 712.

Mack, C., & C. Tama. 1997. *Case Studies as a Means of Exploring Preservice Teachers' Use of Content Area Literacy Strategies in Their Subject Area Field Work.* Scottsdale, AZ: National Reading Conference. ERIC Document Reproduction Service No. ED 417 388.

McCammon, L. A., C. Miller, and J. Norris. 1997. "Using Case Studies in Drama/Theatre Teacher Education: A Process of Bridge Building Between Theory and Practice." *Youth Theatre Journal* 11: 103–112.

———. 1998. "Cacophony and Fugue: Preservice Narratives Create Conversation About Drama Education." *Research in Drama Education* 3(1): 29–44.

———. 1999. "Preservice Drama Teachers as Researchers: Using Case Development and Analysis to Promote the Practice of Research of Research and the Research of Practice." In *Drama and Theatre in Education: International Conversations,* ed. C. Miller and J. Saxton, 40–46. Victoria, BC: The American Educational Research Association Arts and Learning Special Interest Group and the International Drama in Education Research Institute.

———. 1999. "Using Case Narratives in Drama Education to Make

Teaching and Learning Real." *Arts and Learning Research* 15(1): 52–72.

Merseth, K. 1990. "Case Studies and Teacher Education." *Teacher Education Quarterly* 17(1): 53–62.

———. 1994. "Cases, Case Methods, and the Professional Development of Educators." Washington, DC: ERIC Clearinghouse on Teaching and Teacher Education. ERIC Document Reproduction Service No. ED 401 272.

Miller, C., J. Norris, and L. A. McCammon. 1999. "Conversations on the Use of Case Narratives in Drama Methods Classes: A Collaborative Reflective Journey." *Journal of Professional Studies* 7(1): 11–19.

Miller, J. 1992. *Creating Spaces and Finding Voices: Teachers Collaborating for Empowerment*. Albany, NY: State University of New York Press.

Norris, J. 1995. "Pre-Service Drama Teacher Education: Voices from the Practicum." In *Canadian Tertiary Drama Education*, ed. J. Saxton & C. Miller, 59–66. Victoria, BC: University of Victoria.

Norris, J., and L. A. McCammon. 1996. "Using Case Study Narratives in Building Reflective Communities in Pre-Service Teacher Education." Paper presented at the American Education Research Association Conference. New York. ERIC Document Reproduction Service No. ED 401245.

Richards, J. 1996. *Preservice Teachers' Cases in an Early Field Placement*. Charleston, SC: College Reading Association. ERIC Document Reproduction Service No. ED 408 568.

Schank, R. 1990. *Tell Me a Story: A New Look at Real and Artificial Memory*. New York: Scribner's Sons.

Schön, D. 1983. *The Reflective Practitioner*. New York: Basic Books.

Schubert, W., and W. Ayers. 1992. *Teacher Lore: Learning from Our Own Experience*. New York: Longman.

Shulman, J. 1990. "Case Writing as a Site for Collaboration." *Teacher Education Quarterly* 17(1): 63–78.

Shulman, J., ed. 1992. *Case Methods in Teacher Education*. New York: Teachers College Press.

Shulman, L. 1993. "To Reinvent a Pedagogy for Teacher Education." Paper presented at the Western Canadian Conference for Student Teaching, Vancouver, BC.

Silverman, R., W. Welty, and S. Lyon. 1992. *Case Studies for Teacher Problem Solving*. New York: McGraw-Hill.

Valli, L., ed. 1992. *Reflective Teacher Education: Cases and Critiques*. Albany, NY: State University of New York Press.

Wasserman, S. 1993. *Getting Down to Cases: Learning to Teach with Case Studies*. New York: Teachers College Press.

————. 1994. *Introduction to Case Method Teaching: A Guide to the Galaxy.* New York: Teachers College Press.

————. 1994. "Using Cases to Study Teaching." *Kappan* 75(8): 603–11.

Wilson, S. 1989. *A Case Concerning Content: Using Case Studies to Teach Subject Matter.* East Lansing, MI: National Center for Research on Teacher Education. ERIC Document Reproduction Service No. ED 320 851.

Yusko, B. 1997. *Planning and Enacting Reflective Talk Among Interns: What is the Problem?* Chicago: American Educational Research Association. ERIC Document Reproduction Service No. ED 416 735.

Drama Education

Airs, J., and C. Ball. 1995. *Taking Time to Act: A Guide to Cross-Curricular Drama.* Portsmouth, NH: Heinemann.

Boal, A. 1992. *Games for Actors and Non-Actors.* New York: Routledge.

Bolton, G. 1984. *Drama as Education: An Argument for Placing Drama at the Centre of the Curriculum.* Burnt Mill, Harlowe, Essex, UK: Longman.

————. 1992. *New Perspectives on Classroom Drama.* London: Simon & Shuster.

Booth, D. 1994. *Story Drama.* Markham, ON: Pembroke.

Booth, D., and C. Lundy. 1985. *Improvisation.* New York: Harcourt, Brace, Jovanovitch.

Bray, E. 1994. *Playbuilding: A Guide for Group Creation of Plays with Young People.* Portsmouth, NH: Heinemann.

Doyle, C. 1993. *Raising Curtains on Education: Drama as a Site for Critical Pedagogy.* Westport, CT: Burgin and Garvey.

Errington, E. 1993. *Arts Education: Beliefs, Practices and Possibilities.* Geelong, Victoria, Australia: Deakin University Press.

Fleming, M. 1994. *Starting Drama Teaching.* London: David Fulton.

Greene, M. 1995. *Releasing the Imagination: Essays on Education, the Arts, and Social Change.* San Francisco: Jossey-Bass.

Heathcote, D., and G. Bolton. 1995. *Drama for Leaning: Dorothy Heathcotes's Mantle of the Expert Approach to Education.* Portsmouth, NH: Heinemann.

Heathcotte, T. 1994. *Stuff I Wish I'd Known: A Practical Guide for High School Speech and Drama Teachers.* San Diego, CA: Mardel Books.

Heinig, R. 1991. *Improvisation with Favorite Tales: Integrating Drama into the Reading/Writing Classroom.* Portsmouth, NH: Heinemann.

Hobgood, B. 1988. *Master Teachers of Theatre: Observations on Teaching Theatre by Nine American Masters.* Carbondale, IL: Southern Illinois University Press.

Hornbrook, D. 1991. *Education in Drama: Casting the Drama Curriculum.* New York: Falmer Press.

Kempe, A. 1992. *The GCSE Drama Book.* Cheltenham, UK: Simon and Schuster Education.

———. 1997. *The GCSE Drama Book.* 2d ed. Cheltenham, UK: Simon and Schuster Education.

Manley, A., and C. O'Neill. 1997. *Dreamseekers: Creative Approaches to the African American Heritage.* Portsmouth, NH: Heinemann.

Motter, C. 1970. *Theatre in High School: Planning, Teaching, Directing.* Englewood Cliffs, NJ: Prentice Hall.

Neelands, J. 1992. *Learning Through Imagined Experience.* London: Hodders.

O'Neill, C. 1995. *Drama Worlds.* Portsmouth, NH: Heinemann.

Opelt, J. R. 1991. *Organizing and Managing the High School Theatre Program.* Boston: Allyn & Bacon.

O'Toole, J. 1976. *Theatre in Education: New Objectives for Theatre, New Techniques in Education.* London: Hodder & Stoughton.

O'Toole, J., and K. Donelan. 1996. *Drama, Culture and Empowerment.* Brisbane, Queensland: IDEA.

Saldaña, J. 1995. *Drama of Color.* Portsmouth, NH: Heinemann.

Somers, J. 1994. *Drama in the Currciculum.* London: Cassell.

Spolin, V. 1986. *Theatre Games for the Classroom: A Teacher's Handbook.* Evanston, IL: Northwestern University Press.

Tarlington, C., and P. Verriour. 1991. *Role Drama.* Markham, ON: Pembroke.

Tanner, F. A. 1982. *Basic Drama Projects.* 6th ed. Caldwell, ID: Clark Publishing Company.

———. 1982. *Basic Drama Projects—Teacher's Manual.* Caldwell, ID: Clark Publishing Company.

———. 1982. *Creative Communication.* Caldwell, ID: Clark Publishing Company. ISBN 0-931-05440-0.

Taylor, P. 1996. *Researching Drama and Arts Education: Paradigms and Possibilities.* Washington, DC: Falmer Press.

Tomlinson, R. 1982. *Disability, Theatre and Education.* London: Souvenir Press.

Verriour, P. 1994. *In Role.* Markham, ON: Pippin.

Woolland, B. 1993. *The Teaching of Drama in the Primary School.* New York: Longman.

Biographies

Laura A, McCammon, Ed.D., taught speech, drama, and English for fifteen years in Maryville, Tennessee. In 1988 she was named the Outstanding Speech and Drama Educator by the Tennessee High School Speech and Drama League. She is currently the theatre education specialist at the University of Arizona in Tucson, where she teaches creative drama, secondary methods, and supervises student teachers. Her research is in the areas of drama teacher preparation, case-based teaching, and personal story. She won the American Alliance for Theatre and Education Research Award in 1992, 1993, and 1999 and has served as editor for the *Youth Theatre Journal.*

Carole Miller is associate professor and teaches in the elementary and secondary drama in education program in the Department of Curriculum and Instruction at the University of Victoria, British Columbia. She has edited journals in the fields of drama and education and has developed teacher resources for education through drama. She was the cochair with Juliana Saxton of the first National Tertiary Drama Education Conference in Victoria, British Columbia, and the second International Drama in Education Institute. She and Juliana Saxton are co-editors of *Canadian Tertiary Drama Education: Perspectives on Practice; Drama and Theatre in Education: The Research of Practice/The Practice of Research;* and *Drama and Theatre in Education: International Conversations.*

Joe Norris, Ph.D., is professor of drama education at the University of Alberta, where he teaches secondary methods to drama majors and minors. In addition, he teaches courses in theatre in education (TIE) and drama in education (DIE), arts-based educational research, and curriculum theory. He is artistic director of Mirror Theatre, a TIE/DIE troupe that tours shows of an educational and/or social change nature. He was president of the Educational Drama Association of the Nova Scotia Teachers Union, president of the Fine Arts Council of the Alberta Teachers' Association, and the 1998 recipient of the Faculty of Education's Undergraduate Teaching Award.